TARAO GRAMMAR

TARAO
GRAMMAR

By

Chunghkham Yashawanta Singh

AKANSHA PUBLISHING HOUSE
NEW DELHI-110 059 (INDIA)

AKANSHA PUBLISHING HOUSE
R-37B, Vani Vihar, Uttam Nagar,
New Delhi-110 0059 (INDIA)
Phone : 5640621
Email : ektabooks@yahoo.com

Tarao Grammar
First Published 2002
© Author
ISBN 81-87606-16-9

PRINTED IN INDIA

Published by M.P. Misra for Akansha Publishing House, New
Delhi and Printed at Mehra Offset Press, New Delhi.

CONTENTS

ACKNOWLEDGEMENT

It is my long desire to study languages of Manipur, which has 29 different indigenous mother tongues. Manipur has endangered Tibeto-Burman languages or dialects.

For this study I get different helps from different persons and from different sources as well as moral boost. I sincerely thank University Grant Commission (UGC) for giving me the major Project to study the endangered dialects of Manipur.

At last I thank my parent, University of Manipur. I sincerely dedicated to my University, Manipur University.

Ch. Yashawanta Singh

PREFACE

This book is a modest attempt to study the endangered language of the State of Manipur which has 29 other mother tongues. They are not fully or scientifically analyzed.

The book is analyzed in a descriptive model. It has eight chapters. The first chapter deals with phonemes and syllables. The second chapter deals with Noun Categories discussing about Gender, number Case and numerals. The Chapter III discusses about Verb Categories dealing with Verb, concord particle, aspects etc. The chapter IV discusses about Root and Affixation. The chapter deals with word formation. The chapter VI deals with clause structure dealing with simple sentence, complex sentence and compound sentence. The chapter VII discusses about the sentence process i.e., declarative sentence, negation, imperative and interrogative. The book also contents forms of address in chapter VIII. It has also vocabularies in the appendix.

INTRODUCTION

The Taraos are mainly concentrated in the hills of Chandel district. The number of villages have now increased to four. They are Tarao Khullen (Tarao Laimanai), Leishok Ching, Khuringmul and Heikamul with respect to their establishment. The village Heikamul is the latst one which is situated nearby Pallel. About 8 families are still at Shajkeithel (Ukhrul district) where the Tanghkhul Nagas are also inhabiting. Once some of the Tarao families had tried to merge into the Tangkhul Naga. The Taraos are concentrated in Chandel district like the Tanghkul in Ukhrul district.

The Tarao possess a distinct identity wiht reference to other tribe of Manipur. When we trace back their origin we must see into the origin of Old Kuki tribes, because the Taraos are in Old Kuki by the earlier writers (T.C. Hodson, 1908; R.B. Pemberton, 1835; Shakespear, 1912).

The Tarao is one of the oldest tribes in Manipur because they arrived in Tengnoupal area (Manipur) before the 14th century as reported by G. Kabui (1976). Levi-Stranss says:

"Generalized exchanged, in a more or less pure from extends over a vast area of southern Asia. It is found among the so called Old Kuki groups (including the Taraos) of manipur, where although it has been well studied it appears in a form which seems to be very close to that of the Kachin" (1969.269).

The Tarao marriage system is asymmetrical based on external limits of generalized exchange by matrilateral cross-cousin (Mo Br Da) (Bokul Singh, 1999). I tis no longer applicable today. Tarao marriage system was said to be close that of the Kachin Burma and extending a vast of south Asia (Levi-Stranss, 1963).

There are a mainly 6 (six) clans in Tarao. They are (1) Khullen, (2) Katrimsa, (3) Cana, (4) Siloy-Sanei, (5) Mathang-manci and (6) Kahlangsa. There are four sub-clans under Cana clan. They are (i) Leikhan, (ii) Tei-leap, (iii) Sarye and (iv) Thamon.

The main occupation of the Tarao are agriculture, hunting, basket making specially in bamboo and cane works. Comparatively the number of professional holders is quite low though most of them are educated. The whole community of Tarao is adminisered by the traditional village council under a Khulakpa, Head of the village.

The data of this work is collected from Leishokching, and Heikaipokpi 45 km and 30 km respectively from Imphal. The informants are Pishla and Lamtachao.

It is a descriptive grammar of Tarao. It makes an attempt to describe the language from sound system to the sentence level. The book has eight chapters the first chapter deals with south system and syllable. The second and the third chapter deal with Noun categories and Verb categories respectively. The fourth chapter deals with Root and Affixes. Word Formation is discussed in chapter V. The chapter VI deals witht Clause Structure analysing a complex and compound sentences. The chapter VII discusses about Sentences Processes explaining differen aspect of Negation Imperative, Interrogative, Optative and Exclamentary sentences. The last chapter deals with Form of Address in this language.

CHAPTER I
PHONEMES AND SYLLABLE

Tarao has only segmental phonemes, no supra-segmental phonemes like tone and juncture. There are 26 phonemes. The segmental phonemes may be further divided into vowels, consonants and diphthongs. Of 26 phonemes, 20 are consonants; 6 are vowels and 6 are dipthongs. They are discussed in the following relevant sections.

1.1 Vowels

The vowel systems : It is already said that there are 6 vowels in Tarao. They are shown in Table 1. Vowel phonemes are divided into three according to the height of the tongue as high, mid and low.

Chart of vowel phonemes

Front		Central		Back	
Rounded	Un-rounded	Rounded	Un-rounded	Rounded	Un-rounded
	i			u	
	e		∂	o	
			ͻ		

Table 1

Articulatory description of these vowels are given below :

i — High, front, unrounded vowel
e — Mid, front, unrounded vowel
ə — Mid central, unrounded vowel
a — Low central, unrounded vowel
o — Mid, back rounded vowel
u — High, back, rounded vowel

These six vowels are established on the basis of the following minimal pairs.

i/e	:	si	'keep'
		se	'go'
ə/a	:	əy	'bite'
		ay	'crab'
o/u	:	oy	'yes'
		uy	'dog'

More mininal pairs are given here :

a/u	:	kar	'bind'
		kur	'ear'
e/a	:	ce	'paper'
		ca	'tea'
o/a	:	cor	'wet'
		car	'dry'
i/u	:	ni	'two'
		nu	'mother'
u/a	:	khu	'rain'

		kha	'south'
ə/o	:	wən	'belly'
		won	'pot'
o/a	:	thlo	'song'
		thla	month'
ə/u	:	tək	'meat'
		tuk	'find'

Distribution of Vowels

All the six vowels can occur initially, medially and finally. But initial occurrence of /o/ is rare in this language. Their distributions are discussed in the following one by one.

Occurrence of /i/

in	'house'
iŋkhar	'door'
imləy	'tonque'
inti	'gum'
ikbiŋ	'cheek'
ikhuk	'knee'
iril	'intestine'
imlay	'navel'

Medial occurrence :

sil	'cow'
mit	'eye'
thil	'late'

nim	'shadow'
kihu	'wheat'

Final occurrence :

∂kthi	'ugly'
thi	'ginger'
ni	'day'
∂rsi	'star'
khli	'air'
m∂li	'boat'
∂kni	'dream'
si	'keep'

Occurrence of /∂/

Initial occurrence :

∂kcin	'gentle'
∂knu	'future'
∂song	'to enter'
∂koy	'round'
∂sek	'hand'
∂ktem	'to seek'

Medial occurrence :

ph∂r	'mat'
t∂l	'bread'
t∂k	'meat'
b∂ŋ	'wall'
k∂ŋ	'head'
w∂n	'belly'

Final occurrence :

kənə	'disease'
səmudrə	'ocean'
məthlə	'to praise'

Occurrence of /a/

Initial occurrence :

arkhoŋ	'cock'
arpuy	'hen'
arte	'chicken'
aykin	'garden lizard'
arsukma	'oxalis'
ay	'crab'
amu	'seed'

Medial occurrence

baw	'mouth'
kaŋ	'to burn'
naw	'boy'
yak	'blow'
kar	'to kick'
cam	'to wash'
saŋ	'paddy'

Final occuuurence :

əmsa	'not'
əma	'before'

thla	'month'
tilpa	'leech'
tuŋwa	'tomorrow'
nasa	'patient'
∂wa	'river'

Occurrence of /u/

Initial occurrence :

uy	'dog'
uybak	'owl'
ul	'woollen cloth' (wool)
unpa	'elder'
upu	'box'
uytrok	'frog'

Medial occurrence

kum	'year'
kur	'ear'
lut	'shirt'
kut	'hand'
ruy	'to ask'
mul	'hill'
bur	'dust'
hur	'ice'
suŋ	'to pour' (liquid)

Final occurrence

khul	'village'
muju	'rat'

ru	'bamboo'
ǝhu	'stram'
inru	'to steal'
wǝbu	'nest'
mu	'lip(s)'

Occurrence of /o/

Initial occurrence

oy	'yes'

Initial occurrence of /o/ is rare in this language.

Medial occurrence

som	'squeeze'
loy	'journey'
cow	'to dig'
cor	'wet'
noŋ	'cheap'
koy	'break'
lon	'throw'

Final occurrence

makho	'also'
mico	'blind'
sero	'go' (imprerative)
puno	'delay'
mǝco	'to kiss'
thlo	'song'
inlo	'unite'

Vowel Sequence

Vowel phonemes come one after another in disyllabic and trisyllabic words are known as vowel sequence. It is rarely happened in Tarao. Few examples are given below.
Example :

di-in	'day before yesterday'
khi-oŋ	'brick'
mi-in	'today'
ya-ik	'sharp'
thu-enthla	'thunder'
se-uŋ	'go (indefinite form) (simple Present tense)
s∂no-∂ŋ	'do or does not take' negative in Simple Present
tuy-uo-in	'do or does not take (expresses habitual action in Simple Present)
k∂-alt	'to sale'

	i	e	∂	a	u	o
i	√					√
e					√	
∂			√			
a	√					
u		√				
o	√		√		√	

Fig no. Vowel Sequence chart.

The Consonant System
Identification of Consonants

In general consonant can be described and identified by using a three-term labels, indicating whether the sound is voiced or voiceless, the place or point of articulation and the manner of articulation.

In the Table below, consonants are represented on a two dimensional grid. In the grid, the points or place of articulation are set out horizontally and the types of manner of articulation are arranged vertically. The consonant phonemes make distinction between aspirated and unaspirated, voiced and voiceless specially for stops. This is a five-way contrast for stops, namely, bilabial, alveolar, palatal, velar and glottal, nasal is constrated into three, i.e., bilabial, alveolar and velar (see table 2).

p, t, k, c, j	are voicelss unaspirated stops
b, d, g	are unaspirated stops
ph, th, kh	are voicless aspirated stops
m, n, ŋ	are respectively bilabial and alveealar nasals
l	is only palatal lateral
h	is glottal fricatives
r	is palatal trill
w and y	are respectively bilabial and palatal semi-vowels.

Consonant Phonemes

	Bilabial		Alveolar		Palatal		Velar		Glottal	
	Voi ced	V. less	Voi ced	V. less	Voi ced	V. less	Voi ced	V. less	Voi ced	V. less
Stops Aspir ated		ph	d	t	c	j	g	kh		

Unas pi- rated	b	p		th				k		
Fricat ive						s				h
Nasal s	m		n				η			
Latera ls				l						
Trills				r						
Semi- vowel		w		y						

Table 2.

Consonant contrast

These twenty consonants in Tarao are established as different phonemic status on the bais of minimal pair and overlapping pair. For convenient, minimal pairs are given in monosyllabic words. The following examples demonstrate a contrast between two consonants.

Examples :

p/b	:	bucar	'famine'
		puno	'delay'
		∂kpu	'God'
		wabu	'nest'
b/k	:	be	'bean'
		ke	'leg'
c/s	:	ce	'paper'
		se	'go'

r/kh	:	khu	'rain'
		ru	'bamboo'
t/l	:	tək	'meat'
		lək	'lap'
th/s	:	thi	'die'
		si	'keep'
th/l	:	thoy	'cradle'
		loy	'journey'
t/r	:	tuy	'water'
		ruy	'rope'
s/d	:	di	'want'
		si	'keep'
n/th	:	ni	'sun' 'day'
		thi	'die'
m/n	:	mu	'lip' 'sow'
		nu	'mother'

Distribution of Consonants

With the exception of velar stop [g] all the consonants can occur in the initial as well as in the intervocalic positions in a word. But this phoneme [g] is believed to be borrowed from Manipuri which borrowed from Bengali. So it is found in a compound word, **məŋgithəy** (məŋgi + thəy 'fruit).[1]

---

[1] In Manipuri **məŋge** 'tamarine'. In Tarao /e/ of **məŋge** is changed into /i/ i.e., **məŋgi**.

Initial occurrence of the consonants

P	:	pǝt	'cotton'
		pa	'read'
		pot	'thing'
		puno	'delay'
t	:	tuy	'water'
		tilpa	'leach'
		tolthǝy	'guava'
		troŋ	'speak'
k	:	kur	'ear'
		kǝntạ	'bell'
		kopoy	'pomegranet'
		kukthol	'bed'
		kǝla	'distance'
b	:	be	'bean'
		bǝtcọ	'brinjal'
		ben	'brain'
		baw	'mouth'
		bithu	'pea'
d	:	di	'want'
		de-in	'day before yesterday'
		dukan	'shop'
		dǝw	'grass'

ph	:	philcop	'clay'
		phul	'boil'
		phar	'mat'
		phalep	'butterfly'

th	:	thiŋ	'tree'
		thəwcil	'busy'
		thin	dark'
		thum-ənsək	'feed'
		thir	'iron'
		thi	'blood'

kh	:	khamel 'bear'	
		khon	'beat' (v)
		khutmosil	'nail'
		khaw	'grass hopper'
		khuy	'honey bee'

m	:	mətem	'taste'
		mu	'lip'
		məcar	'turn'
		məthəy 'teach'	
		mot	'banana'
		məsəŋ	'answer'
		muju	'rat'

n	:	ni	'day/two'
		nu	'mother, women, aunt'
		na	'ear'
		nar	'nose'
		naw	'boy' (small) 'child'

		nir	'decide'
ŋ	:	ŋəw	'white'
		ŋuŋ	'fly' (v)
		ŋa	'fish'
l	:	leŋ	'game'
		lək	'lap'
		loy	'journey'
		lukhe	'chest'
		laŋtiya	'vulcher'
c	:	cum	'share'
		cəkpol	'soap'
		cor	'wet'
		cəw	'dig'
		cem	'knife'
s	:	som	'squeeze'
		səkte	'some'
		saŋteŋ	'dragon fly'
		suphaytheluk	'pear'
		səysa	'Wednesday'
j	:	jopak	'shield'
h	:	ha	'teeth'
		hur	'ice'
r	:	ruy	'roap'
		rilwol	'love'
		romthok	'glad'
		rəyci	'leprocy'
		rukməy	'gun'

		rukiŋ	'neck'
w	:	wa	'bird'
		w∂n	'belly'
		w∂ntr∂m	'appetite'
		w∂m	'black'
		won	'pet'
		wabu	'nest'
y	:	yokpi	'tiger'
		y∂ŋ	'what'
		yoŋ	'monkey'
		y∂ŋrel/	'why'
		y∂ŋrela	

Medial occurrence

All the twenty consonants can occur in the intervocalic position. But occurrence of the phoneme [g] in a word is very rare. it is already said before.

		kepi	'toes'
p	:	kepi	'toes'
		capla	'glass'
		p∂pok	'Tuesday'
		∂kthop∂y	'drive'
		unpa	'elder'
		ekpe	'give'
t	:	kutpi	'thump'
		th∂ytup	'apple'
		rutuy	'root'
		arte	'chicken'
		b∂tco	'brinjal'

k	:	∂kni	'diamond'
		inkay	'pull'
		∂kir	'piece'
		yokpi	'tiger'
		uyak	'crow'

b	:	inbay	'incline'
		somku	'Ninety'
		somrit	'Eighty'
		uybok	'owl'
		ibuŋ	'skin'

d	:	∂kday	'calm'
		k∂day	'freeze'
		∂ndon	'hope'
		∂duŋ	'sky-blue'
		∂ndi	'little'

ph	:	∂ph∂m	'place'
		∂ph∂ŋ	'solid'
		∂phak	'time'
		saphu	'food'

th	:	∂kthu	'rotten'
		k∂thoy	'proud'
		trongth∂yno	'dump'
		punmuth	'quiet'
		patham	'dagger'
		m∂thup	'hide'

kh	:	∂khum	'spade'
		tuŋkh∂n	'cat'

		inkhar	'door'
		mokhum	'pillow-case'
		lukhe	'chest'
		klukhethuy	'hip'

| g | : | məŋgithəy | 'tarmarine' |

m	:	sumarək	'berry'
		ləymathəy	'appricot'
		rukməy	'gum'
		punmuth	'quiet'
		ənma	'they'

n	:	əntrum	'muster'
		kənta	'bell'
		punsil	'cloth'
		kinita	'oar'
		inti	'gum'
		kəna	'ache'

ŋ	:	koŋru	'backbone'
		thiŋbur	'leaf'
		troŋnir 'oath'	
		saŋteŋ	'dragon fly'
		tuŋwa	'tomorrow'

l	:	nuyləŋ	'plenty'
		inliŋ	'ornament'
		ralmi	'soldier'
		silcol	'bull'
		silte	'calf'

| r | : | khəroy | 'spoon' |

		inru	'steal'
		səwrel	'handicap'
		cirik	'insect'
		sirim	'wild cow'
c	:	məcil	'spit'
		əkcar	'select'
		bucar	'famine'
		incuŋ	'roof'
		silcu	'milk'
s	:	asim	'fun'
		rusum	'grave'
		insoy	'fail'
		masu	'sugar cane'
		əksece	'last'
j	:	injukpe	'insult'
		məyji	'write'
		bəjəŋ	'mirror'
		injuk	'shame'
h	:	əhu	'steam'
		əhəw	'beginning' or 'sound'
w	:	ewonpi	'stomach'
		kuwar	'sky'
		norwal	'snail'
		tuŋwa	'tomrrow'
y	:	lənyom	'save'
		məyan	'yesterday'

kuyar	'sky'
sumyaknəw	'sugar'
əyak	'wake'
rəyya	'one hundred'

Final Occurrence

Of the twenty consonant phonemes, only eight consonants can occur finally. They are p, t, k, m, n, ŋ, r, and l. Examples are given below :

p	:	khantup	'date palm'
		phəlep	'butterfly'
		təp	'slow'
		philcop	'mud' (clay)
		thəytup	'apple'
		mot	'banana'
		lut	'shirt'
		mit	'eye'
		thəi	'kill'
		mit	'eye'

k	:	inthek	'divorce'
		tuk	'find'
		əntak	'wide'
		əpek	'now'
		intuk	'meal'

m	:	kutjom	'gold finger'
		om	'chest'
		inmom	'bud'
		kulum	'warm'
		cam	'wash'
		nim	'image'

n	:	won	'pet'
		inr∂n	'poor'
		∂ksen	'pure'
		∂n	'curry'

l	:	∂knal	'rub'
		c∂kpol	'soap'
		kudol	'rich'
		rilwol	'love'
		∂tul	'liquid'
		thil	'late'

ŋ	:	m∂hoŋ	'open'
		inluŋ	'oppose'
		olay	'noise'
		c∂ŋwaŋ	'marriage'
		kuruŋ	'king'

r	:	∂knur	'next'
		phar	'mat'
		kuyar	'sky'
		khar	'shut'
		nur	'snow'

Consonant Sequence

When two or more consonants are occurred in an immediate position, beyond the syllable it is regarded as consonant sequence. Cluster is known as occurrence of two consonants within a syllable. In other words, briefly, utterance of two sounds at a time. In this language a number of consonants can have immediate occurrence, as given in the following examples.

n : can occur with c, b, j, l, ŋ, th, n, r, w and y

n + c	in-cuŋ	'roof'
	in-cuŋ	'vibrate'
n + b	in-bay	'incline'
n + b	in-bok	'to sit'
n + d	ən-don	'hope'
n + j	in-juk	'shame'
n + l	in-leŋ	'to return'
n + r	in-runi	'theif'
n + r	in-ru	'to steal
n + th	in-thrukna	'origin'
n + th	ən-thlap	'vast'
n + w	sən-wat	'ripe'
n + h	in-hoy	'welt'
n + n	in-nim	'low'
n + ŋ	in-ŋay	'to rest'
n + s	in-sem	'modest'
n + y	in-yom 'save'	

m : can occur with b, c, l, m, n, p, t, y

m + b	əm-brin	'smell'
m + l	in-rom-ləw	'infinite'
m + th	əm-thlah	'step'
m + ch	khəm-cuŋ	'curtain'
m + p	cam-pa	'dagger'
m + t	com-te	'sword'
m + p	com-pa	'dagger'
m + r	əm-ral	'accuse'
m + n	əm-nak	'waist'
m + l	im-ləy	'tougue'
m + y	sum-yaknəw	'sugat'
m + n	sum-nal	'ladies finger'

k : can have an immediate occurrence with c, m, n, l, s, t, th, p, and y

k + th	kuk-thol	'bed'
k + m	ruk-məy	'gun'
k + l	tuk-ləy	'country'

k + c	∂k-ce	'last'
k + n	∂k-nur	'next'
k + t	∂k-ten	'seek'
k + m	∂k-maη	'spoil'
k + l	ph∂k-le	'swallow'
k + s	morok-si	'pepper'
k + y	ik-ya	'arumpit'
k + th	∂k-thra	'good'
k + p	c∂k-poi	'soap'

t : can occur with m, p, j, y and kh.

t + m	kut-m∂ya	'palm'
t + p	kut-pi	'thump'
t + j	kut-jom	'gold finger'
t + y	kut-yuη	'iron finger'
t + m	kut-m∂sil	'nail'
t + kh	mit-khumul	'eye brow'

η can occur with b, c, m, n, p, r, t, η, and w

ŋ + w	tuŋ-wa	'tomorrow'
ŋ + th	troŋ+thəyno	'dump'
ŋ + k	khoŋ+kup	'shoe'
ŋ + c	noŋ+cup	'west'
ŋ + t	noŋ+ta	'your'
ŋ + r	koŋ+ru	'back bone'
ŋ + ŋ	raŋ+ŋa	'five'
ŋ + m	həkcaŋ+mul	'body hair'
ŋ + p	toŋ+pruy	'jute'
ŋ + b	thiŋ+bur	'leaf'
ŋ + w	thiŋ+wuŋ	'root'
ŋ + w	cəŋ+waŋ	'marriage'
ŋ + n	troŋ-nir	'oath'
n + s	troŋ-sən	'say'

l can have an immediate occurrence with c, m, p, t, th and s

l + c	səkol+cuŋ	'riddle'

l + m	ral-mi	'soldeir'
l + s	məlsa	'friend'
l + t	bel-tiŋ	'bucket'
l + th	bel-thuŋ	'pot'
l + p	til-pa	'luch'

r can make a consonant sequence with the phonemes as d, kh, n, p, ph, s and w

r + d	niwar-di	'down'
r + kh	ar-khoŋ	'cock'
r + w	mor-wat	'snail'
r + ph	sər-phok	'tomato'
r - s	ər-si	'star'
r - p	kur-pəŋ	'deap'
r - n	itur-nəŋ	'throat'

There are a few words in which three consonants are occurring immediately i.e., a consonant plus a consonant cluster.

n + r	wəntram	'appetite'

ŋ + tl	kəŋtleŋ	'bald'
n + thl	inthlud	'extinguish'

Consonants Cluster

There are abundant consonant clusters in this language. Consonant clusters are found both in initial and medial positions in monosyllabic, disyllabic and trisyllabic words. But cluster is not found in final syllable. Only one type of cluster is found in this language, i.e., stop + lateral/trill.

Initial occurrence

b + r	:	brina	'cigarette'
t + r	:	troŋ	'word'
t + l	:	tlan	'run'
k + l	:	kluŋ	'diarrhoea'
	:	khukhethuy	'hip'
		khliraŋ	'air'
kh + r	:	khəroy	'spoon'
th + l	:	thla	'month'
		thlam	'cottage'
		thluŋsuk	'swelling'
th + r	:	thransa	'wall lizard'
		thrano	'bad levil'
		thrur	'chase'

Medial Occurrence

Medial occurrence of consonant clusters are found more than initial occurrence and voiced alveolar stop + trill is found in this position but not in initial position.

Example :

b + r	:	əmbrin	'smell'
p + r	:	campra	'lemon
		toŋpruy	'jute'
p + l	:	cəpla	'glass'
d + r	:	indram	'bark'
t + r	:	kutriŋ	'wrist'
		intrim	'combine'
		intruŋ	'flame'
		əntrum	'mustard'
t + l	:	kəŋtleŋ	'bald'
k + l	:	inkle	'bright'
k + r	:	əkrul	'inquire'
th + l	:	əthləŋ	'below'
		məthlap	'fold'
		məthla	'praise'
		əkthləy	'other'

th + r :   əmthru   'invent'
             əkthra   'good'
             ukthru   'pigeon'

Diphthong-like

It is siad already, Tarao has no pure diphthong. But there are some diphthong-like sounds which are not pure diphthong. That is when a semi-vowel follows a pure vowel, a diphthong-like-sound is created as in the given examples :

/əy/   thəypom   'jack fruit'
         thəyno   'unable'
         thəy   'fruit'
         kuməy   'women'
         tukləy   'country'
         imləy   'tongue'
         məywut   'ask'
         rəyci   'leprocy'
         somləyni   'fourteen'

/ay/   kaday   'cold'
         sumphay   'cloud'
         waysi   'danger'
         aykin   'garden lizard'
         nay   'empty'
         tuŋkhay   'half'
         nənkay   'hoise'
         ruŋay   'hear'
         inŋay   'to rest'
         kusay   'elephant'
         kuksay   'spear'

/əw/	ənəw	'yellow'
	thəwcil	'busy'
	thəw	'duty'
	əhəw	'to begin'
	cəw	'dig'
	kəjəw	'harm'
	innəw	'fat'
	kolcəw	'braclet'
	cəwci	'chait'

/oy/	khəroy	'spoon'
	koy	'to break'
	insoy	'fail'
	yopithoyna	'plier'
	loy	'journey'
	əkoy	'round'
	uroy	'to swim'

/uy/	tuy	'water'
	thuy	'hip'
	rutuy	'root' (bamboo)
	tuyba	'tomorrow'
	uyramuy	'fox'
	uyte	'puppy'
	uy-ak	'crow'
	uy	'dog'
	uybək	'owe'

/aw/	naw	'boy'
	thaw	'oil'
	khaw	'grass hopper'
	kəsaw	'anger'
	məthraw	'spread'

A phonetic feature of six vowels of Taraw is shown in the Table No. 3.

	i	e	∂	a	u	o
syllabic	+	+	+	+	+	+
sonorant	+	+	+	+	+	+
consonantal	-	-	-	-	-	-
round	-	-	-	-	+	+
high	+	+	-	-	+	-
back	-	-	+	+	+	+

Table 3. Phonetic Feature of the Vowel Phonemes.

Syllable

A syllable is a vocalic unit or is a unit of pronunciation of a vowel alone or a vowel with one or more consonants.

In this language syllable segment may be divided into three parts : onset, the initial sound or sound occurring before the nucleus i.e. the beginning of a syllable should be a consonant or semi-vowel as in **wa** 'bird' and **be** 'bean'. The central part is the phonetic peak of sonority. It is the nucleus of the syllable and is carried by the vowel not by the consonant. The vowels **o** as in **kor** 'flesh' and 'i' in **nir** 'decide' are the peak of the given mono-syllabic words.

The final sound which comes after the Peak i.e. after the nucleus is called Coda as t in **kut** 'hand' and m in **kum** 'year'. On the other hand a consoant at the end of a syllable is called an arresting consonant, and one in the beginning of a syllable is called a releasing consonant.

The syllabic nucleus is with or without an onset and with or without a Coda. The onset and the coda consist of a single consonant. A syllable which ends in a vowel may be called open and one which ends with a consonant may be called closed (syllables).

Syllabic Pattern

The structures of a syllable can be represented by the formula cvc, where c stands for consonant and v for vowel.

Examples of the some common structure of syllables are cited below :

The Structure of syllable.

Nucleus

cv	se	'walk'	/e/
	di	'want'	/i/
	la	'thread'	/a/
	khu	'village'	/u/
	ke	'leg'	/e/
	thi	'to die'	/i/
	ce	'end'	/e/
	ŋa	'fish'	/a/
vc	∂n	'curry'	/∂/
	ek	'stool/dung'	/e/
	in	'house'	/i/
	in	'sleep'	/i/
	ar	'hen'	/a/
	ul	'wool'	/u/
cvc	bak	'bat'	/a/
	kum	'year'	/u/

kut	'hand'	/u/
cor	'wet'	/o/
hir	'decide'	/i/
lam	'dance'	/a/
mul	'rock'	/u/
wǝn	'belly'	/ǝ/
yǝη	'what'	/ǝ/
khon	'beat'	/o/
sil	'cow'	/i/
tǝk	'meat'	/ǝ/
thiη	'fire-wood'	/i/
ben	'brain'	/e/
phul	'boil'	/u/
pǝt	'cotton'	/ǝ/

Syllable Division

The syllable division depends on preceeding and the following en-vironments of the syllable Peak. Rules of syllablic duration are given below :

v-v	/kǝ-alt/	'sale'
	/khi-oη/	'brick'
	/mi-in/	'today'
	/di-in/	'tomorrow'
	/ya-ik/	'sharp'
	/si-in/	'liver'

v-cv	/ǝ-ma/	'before'
	/ǝ-lu/	'potato'
	/ǝ-wa/	'river'
	/ǝ-mu/	'seed'

cvc-vc   /buŋ-əl/   'wild dog'
             /sil-ek/   'cow dung'
             /ram-uy/   'fox'
             /tuy-in/   'drink'

The following are mono-syllabic words :

1.   mit   'eye'

2.   ke   'leg'

3.   om   'chest'

4.   ni   'sun'

5.   ru   'bamboo'

6.   be   'bean'

7.   nu   'aunt'

8.   ən   'curry'

9.   lə   'song'

10. ha   'teeth'

11. pət   'cotton'

12. kəl   'climb'

13. se   'go'

14. pə   'read'

15. ka   'shoot'

16. kla   'tire'

17. oi   'yes'

18. se   'walk'

19. troŋ   'word'

20. səm   'hair'
21. wən   'belly'
22. thi   'blood'
23. kil   'elbow'
24. ben   'brain'
25. pot   'things'
26. kur   'ear'
27. nar   'nose'

Disyllabic		Trisyllabic	
1. imtei	'tongue'	leimathei	'appricot'
2. im-kha	'chin'	məŋgithei	'tamarine'
3. əkəŋ	'head'	imuŋ məraŋ	'spider'
4. kutsi	'ring'	arsukma	'oxalis'
5. theitup	'apple'	kutməsil	'nail'
6. ərsi	'star'	khlu khe thui	'hip'
7. ku yar	'sky'	niwardi	'dawn'
8. ku sal	'elephant'	kemakhoŋ	'heel'
9. arkho	'cock'	troŋ theiho	'dump'
10. thərah	'mosquito'	sumarek	'berry'
11. morwat	'snail'	uirəmui	'fox'
12. masu	'sugar'	sumyak-nəw	'suger cane'
13. məchi	'salt'	khut məya	'palm'
14. bhusun	'kitchen'	mitnərmul	'eye lash'

15.	nasa	'patient'	məkhəmul	'bear'
16.	ərtui	'egg'	əthəina	'habit'
17.	brina	'cigarrette'	inthrukha	'origin'
18.	kuksai	'spear'	nuithrim	'smile'
19.	belthuŋ	'pot'	əmluitroŋ	'taboo'
20.	rukmei	'gun'	thuenthla	'thunder'
21.	nini	'you'		
22.	imchəl	'forehead'		
23.	kepi	'toes'		
24.	ikhuk	'knee'		
25.	kirit	'eight'		
26.	məsət	'first'		
27.	inlen	'change'		
28.	inchuk	'collide'		

CHAPTER-II
NOUN CATEGORIES

2.1 Noun Categories

In this language, there are two types of nouns. They are (i) Simple noun and (ii) Derived noun. They are discussed in the followings :

(i) Simple noun : are those nouns containing a base only. In other words they are free roots (occurred independently without any affixation), for instances, **khu** 'rain', **tuy** 'water' ∂**wa** 'river' etc.

(ii) Derived noun : are those nouns which are formed by addition of prefix or suffix or by composing two or more roots which cannot occur independently (they are bound roots). So there are two types : affixation and compounding (see for detail in word formation chapter).

Examples :

Affixation

a] troη   'to speak'   troη-m∂oη   'manner of speaking'
   leη   'to play'   leη-m∂oη   'mode of playing'
   [-m∂oη indicates the manner or mode of action]

b] sak   'to eat'   ∂k-sak (mi)   'eater'
   pa   'to read'   ∂k-pa (mi)   'reader'

[ǝk- indicates 'actor' or 'agent', mi 'man']

Compounding :

ru + tuy   >   rutuy   'root'
bamboo water

mit + mul   >   mitmul   'eyebrow'
eye   hair

2.1 Gender

In this language, there is no grammatical gender. But it has natural gender - male and female. In animate nouns, -**puy** and -cǝl are used to indicate male and female respectively. But in the case of the birds the gender difference of male and female are denoted by the suffixes -**khoη** and -**puy** respectively.

Examples :

a] Animals

Male		Female	
silcǝl	'bul'	silpuy	'cow'
uycǝl	'male dog'	uypuy	'female dog'
vokcǝl	'male pig'	vokpuy	'female pig'

b] Birds

arkhoη	'cock'	arpuy	'hen'
usǝk khoη	'male sparrow'	usǝk puy	'female sparrow'
ukthrukhoη	'pigeon' (m)	ukthrupuy	'pigeon' (f)

In human being -**pa** indicates 'male' or 'father' when -**nu** expresses 'female' or 'mother.'

2.2 Number

Like gender, Tarao has no grammatcal agreement in Number. The most common manifestion is the distribution between singular and plural which rest upon recognition of person, animals and objects. There are three different morphemes for indicating plural. They are -**ni**, -**ən** and -**əy**.

The plural morpheme -**ni** occurs with first person and second person personal pronouns while the morpheme **ən**- is prefixed to the third person personal pronoun to make a plural form. The other morpheme -**əy** is suffixed to the nouns only.

Pronoun

	Singular		Plural	
kəy	'I'	kəy-ni	'we'
nəŋ	'you'	nəŋ-ni	'you'
əma	'he'	ən-ma	

Noun

wa	'bird'	wa-əy	'birds'
mi	'person'(man)	mi-əy	'persons' (men)
naw	'child'	naw-əy	'children'

Not only the above manifestation of number difference, the 'collective' or 'group' nouns also are found in this language. It is indicated by the suffixes -**bom** and -**rul**. The suffix -**rul** is used with human being while -**bom** is used with non-human beings.

Example

-rul : used in human being

Singular		Plural	
kum∂y	'woman'	kum∂y-rul	'woman + collective'
naw	'child'	naw-rul	'child + collective'
mi	'man'	'mi-rul	'man + collective'

-bom : used in non-human being

uy	'dog'	uy-bom	'dog + collective'
wa	'bird'	wa-bom	'bird + collective'
sa	'animal'	sa-bom	'animal + collective'

2.3 Case

Case is an important inflectional category of noun. Case show the relation between noun and verb and between the two nouns (in the case of genitive). There are seven case markers. They are :

Nominative	n∂ ~ inn∂
Accusative	t∂
Genitive	w∂
Instrumental	inn∂
Locative	niŋŋ∂~∂
Associative	so
Ablative	n∂t∂

Nominative

The most widely accepted function of the nominative is to mark the subject of the sentence.

Example :

1] tomba-nə   la   əthlok-tu
   Tomba-nom. song sing-unreal.
   'Tomba will sing a song'

2] əma-nə layrik khət əkləy-pəy
   he-nom. book   one buy-perf.
   'He has brought a book'

Accusative

It is used to make the object of a trnasitive verb.
Example :

3] əma-nə inni-tə   iŋlis   məthəy-tuŋ
   he-nom. we-accu. English teach-unreal.
   'He will teach us English'

4] kəy-innə əmə-tə   ki-ən
   I-nom.   he-accu. 1pp. look
   'I look at him'

Genetive

It is the case possession of something. Example :

5] kəy tomba-wa   ə-pa   ki-rom
   I   Tomba-gen.   3pp. father 1pp-know

'I know tomba's father'

6] əmay nəŋ-wa ə-in
this you-gen 3pp. house
'This is your house'

Instrumental

It is used to indicate 'with which' somthing is done (used as an intrument). The marker is homophonous to nominative marker. Example :

7] ənma rəy-innə thiŋ ətən
they axe-inst. tree cut
'They cut the tree with an axe'

8] kəy-innə ce ki-təŋ-məŋuŋ
I scissor-inst. paper cut-prog.
'I cut the paper with a scissor'

Locative

It marks the location of both special and temporal reference, and location of something to a place. The marker is suffixed to place aid time. The marker -**niŋŋa** occurs with human beings whle -ə occurs elsewhere.

Example :

9] kəy səkul-ə se-tuŋ
I school-loc. go-unreal.
'I will go to school'

10] kəy-innə kəythil-ə se-tuŋ

I-nom. market-loc. go-unreal.
'I will go to market'

11] thimji-khə cawba-niŋŋa pe-ro
book-det. chaoba-dat. give-comd.
'Give the book to Chaoba'

Associative

The marker -**so** marks the sense of 'company with'.
Example :

12] kəy ki-ute-so kəythil-ə se-tuŋ
I sister-asso. market-loc. go-unreal.
'I will go to market with my sister'

13] yayma tomba-so thleŋ-tu
Yaima Tomba-asso. come-unreal.
'Yaima will come with Tomba'

14] kay tomba-so ki-thimji ki-pa
I Tomba-asso. book 1pp. read
'I read the book with tomba'

Ablative

The marker is -**nətə** which markes separation from a
source. Example :

15] kəy əwa-nətə tuy ki-coy
I river-abl. water 1pp. fetch
'I fetch water from the river'

16] kəni-innə   sil-nətə   cu kən-som
we-nom.   cow-abl. milk 1pp. milking
'We milk the cow'

17] yayma dili-nətə   thleŋ-tu
Yaima Delhi-abl. come-perf.
'Yaima will come from Delhi'

It is learnt that there are seven case markers in this language. The question of ergativity does not arise in this language; more and above, nominative marker is not obligatory even in the case of transitive sentence.

2.4 Numeral

In the Tarao numeral system here, it is confined only to the cardinal, ordinal numbers and their formations. In the Tarao cardinal systems, namely, addition and multiplication are employed. The term decade is used for the formation of multiplication compounds.

The followings are the basic cardinal numerals of Tarao.

inkhət	'one'
ini	'two'
inthum	'three'
mənli	'four'
raŋŋa	'five'
kuruk	'six'
siri	'seven'

kirit	'eight'
ku	'nine'
som	'ten'

From 11 to 19 are formed by using the dacade work som 'ten' and lǝy 'plus' and the basic numeral 1-9, as in the following.

somlǝy inkhǝt	'eleven'
somlǝy ini	'twelve'
somlǝy inthum	'thirteen'
somlǝy mǝnli	'fourteen'
somlǝy raŋŋa	'fifteen'
somlǝy kuruk	'sixteen'
somlǝy siri	'seventeen'
somlǝy kirit	'eighteen'
somlǝy ku	'nineteen'

The compound numerals denoting 20, 30, 40, 50, 60, 70, 80 and 90 are formed by the use of decade term som multiplied by the basic cardinal numerals, 2, 3, 4, 5, 6, 7, 8, and 9 respectively as in the following examples :

somni	10 x 2 = twenty
somthum	10 x 3 = thirty
somli	10 x 4 = forty
somŋa	10 x 5 = fifty
somruk	10 x 6 = sixty

somsiri	10 x 7 = seventy
somrit	10 x 8 = eighty
somku	10 x 9 = ninety

In Tarao, from 11-19, 21-29, 31-39, 41-49, 51-59, 61-69, 71-79,. 81-89 and 91-99 are additive compounds. Additive compounds are formed by addition involving decade numerals, multiplicative compounds and basic numerals. They use a marker ləy as an additive marker. Briefly the decades are given in the following.

a] from 11-19   somləy inkhət   'eleven'
                 somləy ini   'twelve'
                 somləy inthum   'thirteen'

b] from 21-29   somniləy inkhət   'twenty one'
                 somniləy ini   'twenty two'
                 somniləy inthum   'twenty three'

c] from 31-39   somthumləy inkhət   'thirty one'
                 somthumləy ini   'thirty two'
                 somthumləy inthum   'thirty three'

d] from 41-49   somliləy inkhət   'forty one'
                 somliləy ini   'forty two'
                 somliləy inthum   'forty three'

e] from 51-59   somrukləy inkhət 'fifty one'
                 somrukləy ini   'fifty two'
                 somrukləy inthum 'fifty three'

f] from 61-69   somrukləy inkhət 'sixty one'
                 somrukləy ini   'sixty two'

	somruklǝy inthum	'sixty three'
g] from 71-79	somsirilǝy inkhǝt	'seventy one'
	somsirilǝy ini	'seventy two'
	somsirilǝy inthum	'seventy three'
h] from 81-89	somritlǝy inkhǝt	'eighty one'
	somritlǝy ini	'eighty two'
	somritlǝy inthum	'eighty three'
i] from 91-99	somkulǝy inkhǝt	'ninety one'
	somkulǝy ini	'ninety two'
	somkulǝy inthum	'ninety three' etc.

Ordinal numerals

A number to indicate order as position such as a specific seat in a raw. In other words, it refers to the class of numerals - first, second, third, etc. by contrast with the cardinal numbers one, two, three etc.

In Tarao, ordinal numbers are formed by suffixing <u>tipi</u> to the cardinal numbers as illustrated below :

inkhǝt tipi	'first'
ini tipi	'second'
inthum tipi	'third'
mǝnli tipi	'fourth'
raŋŋa tipi	'fifth'
kuruk tipi	'sixth'

siri tipi   'seventh'

kirit tipi   'eight'

ku tipi   'ninth'

som tipi   'tenth'

The term indicating once (one time), twice (two times), thrice (three times) etc. in the language are formed by prefixing wəy to the cardinal number as in the following examples :

wəyinkhət   'once'

wəyini   'twice'

wəyinthum   'thrice'   etc.

CHAPTER III
VERB CATEGORIES

3.1 Verb

A verb is an important componant in a sentence. It can be divided into three main types, namely, (a) action verb, (b) process and (c) stative verb in Tarao.

Action verb

in	'drink'
lon	'throw'
sak	'eat'
kaw	'kick'
se	'go'
nir	'stand'
tlan	'run'
ruy	'laugh'

Process verb

sun	'cook'
sem	'prepare'
min	'ripe'
raŋ	'blow'

Stative verb

∂k-rik	'to be heavy'
∂k-day	'to be cold'
∂k-rol	'to be big'
∂k-di	'to be small'
∂k-thra	'to be nice or good'

(**∂k-** is used to form adjective)

3.2 Concord particles

Tarao has concord particles occurring with the first person, second person and third person, that is, the particle ∂η occurs with the first person; **ce** with the second person. With the third person a suffix -**i** is used, different from the two previous particles, that is it is a suffix as well as it (-**i**) is suffixed to the noun (subject). The concords function as verb be in the equative sentences.

Examples :

1] k∂y d∂kt∂r ∂η
   I   doctor be
   'I am a doctor'

2] n∂η d∂kt∂r ce
   'You are a doctor'

3] ∂ma-i d∂kt∂r
   he be doctor
   'He is a doctor'

4] məy-i uy
this be dog
'This is a dog'

5] məkha-i rəmuy
that be fox
'That is a fox'

3.3 Auxiliary verb

In this language there are only three auxiliary verbs. They are **cek** 'can', **ce** 'do' and əya 'may'. They are discussed one by one :

Additional sentence

a] nəw bu ə-sak cek
child rice 3pp. eat can
'The child can eat rice'

b] əma eŋlis ə-troŋ cek
he English 3pp. speak can
'He can speak English'

(a) **cek** 'can'

6] kəy pʰur cek-no
I carry can-neg.
'I cannot carry'

7] əma uhleŋ cek
he come can
'He can come'

8]   kǝy phur cek-no-tuŋ
     I carry can-neg. fut.
     'I will not be able to carry'

9]   ǝma kleŋ cek-no-tu
     he come can-neg. fut.
     'He will not be able to come'

10] kǝy mǝji cek-no-tuŋ
     I write can-neg.-fut.
     'I will not be able to write'

The auxiliary **cek** 'can' follows the verb, in the sence that it **cek** ends sentence.

(b) **ce** 'do'

It is used as axiliarly in the interrogative sentence, as in the following sentences :

11] khleŋ ce-me
     come do-q.mk.
     'do you come ?'

12] nǝŋ bu ni-sak ce-me
     you rice 2pp. eat do q.mk.
     'Do you eat rice?'

(c) **ǝya** 'may'

The auxiliary verb **ǝya** occurs like **cek** 'can' and **ce** 'do' after the main verb.

13] kəy khleŋ əya
 I   come may
 'I may come'

14] əma khleŋ əya
 he come may
 'He may come'

3.4 Transitive and Intransitive

The question of ergativity does not arise in this language, i.e., there is no additional marker suffixed to the subject of the transtive verb. This can be clear from the following transtitive and intransitive sentences.

Transitive Sentence

15] kəy-ta əmertha uy   inŋəw inthum əm
 I-gen nice   dog white. three have
 'I have three nice white dog'

16] kəy yukpi khə ki-mu
 I tiger one !pp. see
 'I see a tiger'

17] əma bu   ə-sak
 he rice 3pp. eat
 'He eats his meal'

Intransitive Sentence

18] wa kejuŋ
 bird fly
 'Birds fly'

19] kəy se əŋ
 I   go
 'I go'

20] ənma nuy uŋ
 they laugh
 'They laugh'

3.5. Aspect

In Tibeto-Burman tense, in general, is not distinctive, like other TB languages Tarao has no tense : aspect in more predominent. The following sentences substaintiate that Tarao has no tense.

21] kəy yukpi khət ki-mu
 I   tiger one 1pp. see
 'I see a tiger'

22] kəy miyan yukpi khət ki-mu
 I yesterday tiger one 1pp. see
 'Yesterday I saw a tiger'

The time reference **miyan** 'yestertday' does not force entity to be added to the verb or doest not force to bring in a new entity in the construction. In other word, in the above two sentences the verb **ki-mu** 'see' remains the same.

There are some morphomes, that is, -əy indicating 'continuous'; cepəy indicating 'completed' and **tu/tuŋ** indicating future (unrealise). It will be more convenient to talk on **Aspect** not on tense in Tarao. This concept is actually against the concept of Traditional grammerians. Tarao has four aspects :

I. Simple aspect - expressing simple statement, habitual meaning, routine action.

II. Imperfective aspect - a going on action (Imperfect).

III. Perfective aspect - the action has already completed.

IV. Unrealized aspect - performing the action or event in the near future i.e., the action is not realized yet (it is also known as Irrealis).

They are discussed below :

I. Simple Aspect

It is expressed by the zero morpheme and it is learnt also that Tarao is a verbal prominalized language. Simple aspect is indicated by Pronominal Prefix plus verb. It will be seen from the following sentences.

1] kəy bu ki-sak
   I   rice 1pp. eat
   'I eat rice'

2] əma   la   ə-thok
   She/he song 3pp. sing
   He/she sings a song'

3] kəy yukpi khət ki-mu
   I   tiger one 1pp. see
   'I see a tiger'

4] əma layrik rəŋa əkləy
   he book five 3pp. buy

'He buys five books'

II. Imperfective aspect

It express the action is continuing or progressing. It has three lingusitic entity. The imperfective aspect is formed by using a lexical item **m∂ŋ∂y** which occurs after the verb.

5] ∂nma leŋ   m∂ŋ∂y
   they play prog.asp.
   'They are playing'

6] ∂nma la   ∂thlok m∂ŋ∂y
   they song 3pp. sing   prog.asp.
   'They are singing'

7] k∂y bu kitsak m∂ŋ∂y
   'I am taking rice/meal'

But when the action is done with or inclusive of the speaker then another lexical item **m∂ŋuŋ** is used to indicate the action is going on. Example :

8] k∂-ni leŋ   m∂ŋuŋ
   we   play pro.asp.
   'We are playing'

9] k∂-ni sinema ∂n-se m∂ŋuŋ
   we   cinema go   prog.asp.
   'We are going to cinema'

10] k∂-ni bu ki-sak m∂ŋuŋ
    'We are taking rice/meal'

11] kə-ni layrik khət pə məŋuŋ
    we   book   me read prog. asp.
    'We are reading a book'

Progressive is also expressed by a suffix -əy specially after the lateral **l** and nasal **n**, as in the following examples.

12] ənma thiŋ tən-əy
    they tree cut-prog.mk.
    'They are cutting tree'

13] ənma ənul kəl-əy
    they hill climp-prog.mk.
    'They are climbing hill'

III. Perfect aspect

This is expressed by lexical item **cepəy** which occurs after the main verb. Examples are given in the followings.

14] kəy bu ki-sak cepəy
    I   rice 1pp. eat perf. mk.
    'I have taken my meal'

15] kəni sinema kən ən cepəy
    we   cinema   see perf.mk.
    'We have seen the picture'

16] kəni tomba-tə   khət məna pek cepəy
    we   Tomba acc.mk/dat/ one reward give perf.mk.
    'We have given Tomba a reward'

IV. Unrealized or Irrelais

This is expressed by the suffix -tu or **tuη** in this language. The suffix -**tu** occurs with the second person and third persons whereas the suffix **tuη** occurs with the first person.

Example :

17] kəy bu sak-tuη
    I   rice eat-unrea.mk.
    'I shall eat rice'

18] kəni sinema ən-tuη
    we cinema see-unrea.mk.
    'We will see a cinema'

19] thoybi la   thlok-tu
    Thoibi song sing-unrea.mk.
    'Thoibi will sing a song'

20] əma layrik khət ləy-tu
    he book one buy-unrea.mk.
    'He will buy a book'

CHAPTER IV
ROOT AND AFFIXES

4.1 Root

This is that part of the word which is remained when all the affixes have been removed.

The root can be classified into two as : (i) free root and (ii) bound root.

In this language the free roots can be found in monosyllabic, disallabic and polysyllabic words.

Free root

a. Monosyllabic free root

ha	'teeth'
wa	'bird'
uy	'dog'
kut	'hand'

b. Disyllabic free root

ərsi	'star'
əma	'he'
kənta	'bell'
bətir	'thatch'

c. Polysyllabic free root

kutməsil	'nail'
sumyaknəw	'sugar'
indənnə	'fort'
thuenthla	'thunder'

Bound roots

Bound roots are those which can not occur independently nor it can function as a noun or nominal in any circumtances without the help of an affix or affixes as ə-in əhaw, ə-in koy etc. The prefix ə- indicates third person pronominal marker. After the prefixation of ə- entity gives conceivable meaning. Abundant examples are given below:

Examples :

ə + haw	>	əhaw	'begining'
ə + koy	>	əkoy	'top'
ə + kon	>	əkon	'nest'
ə + juŋ	>	əjuŋ	'root'
ə + kir	>	əkir	'pieces'
ə + pul	>	əpul	'bundle'
ə + kom	>	əkom	'border or bank'
ə + na	>	əna	'leaf'
ə + mor	>	əmor	'tip'

The prefix ∂- is very much similar to Manipuri **m∂-**. Example :

m∂kon	'nest' (his)
m∂pun	'bundel'
m∂ton	'tip'

4.2 Affixes

Affixes are bound morpheme which can only attached to a root or stem or word. In an agglulinative language, affixes are very important. They take in the formation of various words and in deriving several word class, namely verb, noun, adjective etc. Besides these, they are used in forming various sentence types – declarative, negative, ineterrogative and imperative.

In Taroa, there are two types of affixes – Prefixe and Suffix. Infix is not found in this language as it (infix) is not found in Tibeto-Burman languages. They are discussed in the following.

4.2.1 Prefixes

In this language, there are certain prefixe. They are (a) Pronominal prefixe, (b) Reflexive prefix, (c) Causative prefix, (d) Benefactive prefix, (e) Recipocal prefix, (f) Intensive prefix and (g) Directional prefix. They are discussed one by one in the following.

a. Pronominal prefixes

There are three pronominal prefixes in Tarao. They are **ki-** for first person, **ni-** for second person ans **ə-** for third person. The first person pronominal prefix (1pp) is derived from the first person pronoun **kəy** 'I'. In the same manner the prefix **ni-** 'second person pronominal' (2pp) and **ə-** third person pronominal prefix (3pp) are derived from the second and third person pronoun **nəη** 'you' and **əma** 'he/she' respectively.

Example :

ki + pa	>	kipa		'my father'
ni + pa	>	nipa		'you father'
ə + pa	>	əpa		'his/her father'

other examples are :

kisəm	'my hair'
kisa	'my son'
kikut	'my hand'
nikəη	'your head'
nikhu	'you village'
əkəη	'his/her head'
əin	'his/her house'

b. Reflexive prefix

In this language, reflexive 'oneself' is indicated by a prefix **ki-** by adding to an action verb.

Examples :

1] sak   'eat'   ki-sak   'to eat oneself'

2] m∂tha 'to send'   ki-m∂tha 'to send oneself'

3] kheŋ   'to come'   ki-kheŋ   'to come oneself'

4] pa   'to read'   ki-pa   'to read oneself'

c. Causative prefix

In this language, causative is formed by prefixing a morpheme **kim-** to the verb, as shown in the following examples :

1] troŋ   'to speak'   kim-troŋ   'cause to speak'

2] pa   'to read'   kim-pa   'cause to read'

3] lon   'to throw'   kim-lon   'cause to throw'

4] tlan   'to run'   kim-tlan   'cause to run'

d. Benefactive prefix

Benefactive is indicated by addition of a prefix **k∂m-** to the verb, as in the following examples.

1] sak 'to eat' kəm-sak 'to eat for some one'

2] in 'to drink' kəm-in 'to drink for some one'

3] kəl 'to climb' kəm-kəl 'to climb for some one'

e. Intensive prefix

A prefix **khəlmo-** is prefixed to the verbal root to indicate the intensive degree of meaning in this language. It expresses intensive degree of an action performed by an agent, as in the following examples :

1] khəlmo-tlan 'to run very fast'

2] khəlmo-in 'to drink very much'

3] khəlmo-ən 'to look very sharply'

4] kəlmo-inrol 'to become very big'

f. Directional prefix

In this language, the two directions 'up' and 'down' are indicated by the prefix **həŋ-** and **yuŋ-** respectively.

Examples :

həŋ 'up'

1] həŋ-tlan 'to run upward'

2] həŋ-ŋəŋ to fly up'

3] hǝŋ-kaw   'to kick up'

4] hǝŋ-mǝhar   'to turn-up'

    yuŋ   'down'

1] yuŋ-ro   'turn down'

2] yuŋ-tlan   'to run down ward'

3] yuŋ-suŋ   'to pour down'

4] yuŋ-yal   'to blow down'

Besides these prefixes, there are some suffixes which indicate direction. They are discussed in the suffix sections.

Besides these, there are two other prefixes which are used in the formation of new word, say in noun formation. The two prefixes are ǝ- and kǝ- which are used to derive noun; ǝ- is added to action verb while kǝ- is added to stative verb.

Examples :

kǝ-

1] kǝ + traŋ   >   kǝtraŋ   'to be strong'

2] kǝ + yaŋ   >   kǝyaŋ   'to be fast'

ǝ-

1] ǝ + kǝl   >   ǝkǝl   'climber'

2] ∂ + sak > ∂sak 'eater'

3] ∂ + pa > ∂pa 'reader'

Among the prefixes, pronominal prefix is the only one nominal prefix while others like, reflexive, causative, benefactive, intensive and directional are verbal prefixes.

4.2.2 Suffixes

The affixes which can occur after the root are known as sufixes. In agglutinative language, there are many prefixes and suffixes. In this language also, there are many suffixes which are more than the number of prefixes. For convenient in our analysis, they can be categorised into two groups, such as (a) nominal suffixes and (b) verbal suffixes. They are discussed one by one in the following.

a. Nominal suffixes

Nominal suffixes are very large in number they are plural markers, dimunitive marker, case markers, demonstrative markers, gender markers.

1. Gender markers

There are two different sets of suffixes to indicate male and female : for the animal -c∂l and -**puy** are used to express male and female; for the bird the suffix -**khoη** and -**puy** are used to express male and female respectively. (see for detail in Gender)

Male		Female	
silcəl	'bull'	silpuy	'cow'
arkhoŋ	'cock'	arpuy	'hen'

For expressing common gender a suffix -**te** is used [-**te** indicates small]

sil-te	'calf'
uy-te	'puppy'

2. Number suffix

For indicating plural Taroa uses a suffix -**əy** and for collective noun -**rul** to human being while -**bom** to animal are used. (see for detail in Number).

uy	'dog'	uy-əy	'dogs'
thiŋ	'tree'	thiŋ-əy	'trees'

Collective noun

uy	'dog'	uy-bom	'dog + collective'
mi	'man'	mi-rul	'men + collective'

Case suffix

In this language there are seven case suffixes. They are:

Nominative marker	nə/inə

Accusative	tə
Genitive	wa
Instrumental	innə
Locative	niŋə/ə
Associative	so
Ablative	nətə

Demonstrative -khə, -i

The demonstrative marker in this language is a suffix.

naw	'child'	naw-khə	'child-dem.'

thiŋ	'tree'	thiŋ+i	'tree + this'

In this language the expressions of place and directions are made by adding certain affixes to the nominal basis. These affixes indicate the exact location. Examples of such nominal or noun suffixes are given below :

-cuŋ	'on or above'
-suŋ	'in or inside'
-pal	'out or outside'
-əthuy	'below or under'

Suffixes with the nouns are given below :

-cuŋ	'on or above'

ləm	'road'	ləp-cuŋ	'on or above a road'

in	'house'	in-cuŋ	'on or above a house'
phar	'mat'	phar-cuŋ	'on or above a mat'
he	'head'	lu-cuŋ	'on or above a head'

-suŋ	'in or inside'		
tom	'store'	tom-suŋ	'in a store'
in	'house'	in-suŋ	'in or inside a house'
bel	'pot'	bel-suŋ	'in or inside a pot'
bukaŋ	'basket'	bukaŋ-suŋ	'in or inside a basket'

-pal	'out or outside'		
skul	'school'	skul-pal	'outside a school'
in	'house'	in-pal	'outside a house'
dukan	'shop'	dukan-pal	'outside a shop'

-∂thuy	'below or under'		
k∂ŋthol	'bed'	k∂ŋthol-∂thuy	'below/under a bed'
thiŋ	'tree'	thiŋ-∂thuy	'below/under a tree'
teb∂l	'table'	teb∂l-∂thuy	'below/under a table'

Exclusiveness

The suffix -**rut∂** is added to a noun to indicate 'only'.

Examples :

∂n-rut∂	'only curry'
ru-rut∂	'only bamboo'
inl∂w-rut∂	'only grass'
mici-rut∂	'only salt'
cem-rut∂	'only knife'
kuksay-rut∂	'only spear'

Verbal suffixes

There are some verbal suffixes. They are aspect, mood and sentence markers (negative marker, imperative marker, interrogative markers).

a. Aspect markers

Aspect markers are the suffixes in the language. They are

Simple aspect	- φ (pronominal + verb root)
Progressive aspect	- m∂yuŋ ~ m∂ŋ∂y ~ ∂y ~ m∂ŋuŋ
Perfect aspect	- cep∂y ~ p∂y
Unrealised aspect (irrealis)	- tu ~ tuŋ

(see for detail in Aspect)

b. Mood markers

There are five mood markers. They are

1. Dissatisfied mood   -ləwa
2. Potential mood   -cek
3. Probability mood   -kikdet
4. Surprise mood   -so

(see for detail in Mood)

c. Sentence markers

Different types of sentence, such as Negation, Imperative and Interrogative are formed by adding respective markers. They are the suffixes. They are :

Negation   -no

Imperative   -ro

Interrogative   -me

(see for detail in respective sections)

Besides all these suffixes, there is one suffix -**sa** which has multifarious functions and provides different meaning under different circumstances in this language. The suffix -**sa** basically functions as auxiliary as well as 'be' verb in different situations.

a] -**sa** performing as verb 'be' as in the following examples.

    1] əma doctor-sa
        he   doctor-be
        'He is a doctor'

    2] tomba oja-sa
        Tomba teacher-be

'Tomba is a teacher'

b] when the suffix -**sa** occurs with the unrealised aspect marker -**tuŋ** it gives the meaning of 'near future', as in the examples :

    3] thleŋ-tuŋ-sa
       come -un.real.
       'Will/shall come'

c] When the command marker -**re** occurs with -**sa**, it gives the meaning of 'prohibitive'.

    4] doŋ-re-sa
       'Stop it' (formal form)

d] -**sa** is also used in optative to express a wish

    5] ki leŋ-ya-sa
       I   play-NZP-
       'I wish to play'

e] It is also used in exclamatory sentence.

    6] ∂s pote uk-∂thra-sa   [∂ thra-sa 'a nice thing]
       'How wonderful is this !'

f] -**sa** indicates an action 'that is still going on' or about a person expressing how he spends the last time.

    7] pa-l∂w   ∂m-sa
       read-part. spend-
       'He was spending the time by reading'

8] leŋŋa-ləw əm-sa
sing part. spend
'He was spending by singing'

g] When -**sa** occurs with **ci**- it gives the meaning of a complete action. (perfect)

9] la-kha ci-sa
son det. end
'The song has ended'

10] layrik-kha maŋ-sa
book det. lost
'The book has been lost'

11] əma əse-sa
he go
'He has gone'

12] thiŋ-kha kik-sa
tree det. break
'The tree has been broken'

CHAPTER V
WORD FORMATION

In word formation, there are two strategies. They are affixation and compounding. They are discussed one by one in the followings.

5.1 Affixation

Formation of words through the addition of affixes is termed as affixation. In affixation, in this language there are two processes for formation of word –prefixation and suffixation.

Prefixation

In Tarao there are only two prefixes -∂ and k∂- which are added to the root to derive a word. By their prefixation, the word class is changed.

Example :

	Verb	Noun
∂--	∂ + kal 'climb'	∂k∂l 'climber'
	∂ + pa 'read'	∂pa 'reader'

ə + sak   əsak
   'eat'   'eater'

kə-   kə + trəŋ   kətrəŋ
       'strong'   'to be strong'

kə + yaŋ   kəyaŋ
   'fast'   'to be fast'

There is another prefix ək- which is prefixed to form adjective in Tarao.

Examples :

sak   'eat'

1]   sak ək-saka mi   →   əksak mi
      eat   man
      'The man who eats' (eater)

2]   in ək+in mi   →   əkin mi
      drink
      'The man who drinks' (drinker)

3]   pa ək+pa mi   →   əkpa mi
      read
      'The man who reads' (reader)

4]   lam ək +lam mi   →   əklam mi
      dance
      'The man who dances' (dancer)

Other than these prefixes are the pronominal prefixes. They are **ki-** first person, **mi-** second person ə- third person.

These pronominal prefixes are used in kinship reference as well as addressing terms.

pa   'father'   ki + pa   > kipa   'my father'

                 ni + pa   > nipa   'your father'

                 ∂ + pa   > ∂pa   'his father'

These pronominal markers are also used in referring to the body parts.

s∂m 'hair'   ki + s∂m   > ki-s∂m   'his hair'

kut 'hand'   ni + kut   > ni-kut   'your hand'

Not only the prefixes, there are also some suffixes which involved in word formation also. They are gender markers (**c∂l** 'male, **-puy** 'female), diminutive suffix **-te**, and for making manner of noun **-m∂oŋ**.

Example :

c∂l 'male', -puy   'female'

sil-c∂l	>	silc∂l	'bull'
sil-puy	>	silpuy	'cow'
uy + c∂l	>	uyc∂l	'dog' (M)
uy + puy	>	uypuy	'dog' (F)

Diminutive marker -te 'small'
Examples :

sil + te   >   silte   'calf'

uy + te   >   uyte   'puppy'

Manner of Noun

It is expressed by suffixation of -m∂oŋ.

Example :

troŋ	'speak'	troŋ-m∂oŋ	'the manner of speaking'
leŋ	'play'	leŋ-m∂oŋ	'the mode of playing'
tlan	'run'	tlan-m∂oŋ	'manner of running'
sak	'eat'	sak-m∂oŋ	'manner of eating'
pa	'read'	pa-m∂oŋ	'manner of reading'

5.2 Compounding

It is one of the strategies for the formation of new words in which words are formed by combination of two or more roots. There may be combination of noun + noun or noun + verb or noun + adjective. They are discussed in the followings :

a. Noun + Noun

In this category nouns are formed with the combination of another noun. They are illustrated below :

Examples :

1] ru + tuy   >   rutuy   'root'
bamboo water

2]	mit + mul	>	mitmul	'eyebrow'
	eye hair			

3]	sil + ek	>	silek	'cowdung'
	cow dung			

4]	sil + tək	>	siltək	'beef'
	cow fresh			

5]	əntrum + thaw	>	əntrum	'thaw'
	mustard oil			

b. Noun + Adjective

In this category nouns are formed with the combination of an adjective.

Examples :

1]	sil + te	>	silte	'calf'
	cow small			

2]	nu + te	>	nute	'cousin (sister)'
	aunt small			

3]	kur + pəŋ	>	kurpəŋ	'deaf'
	ear foolish			

4]	uy + te	>	uyte	'puppy'
	dog small			

5]	məthəŋ + kum	>	məthəŋ	'next year'
	next year			

c. Adjective + Noun

1] ǝksece + kum   >   ǝksecekum   'last year'
   last   year

2] mǝthǝŋ + thla   >   mǝthǝŋthla   'next month'
   next   month

3] kǝday + thla   >   kǝdaythla   'next winter'
   to be cold month

There is a different type of compounding, I called it, Opaque compounding, because underlying meaning is not possible to establish from two words. In other words, there is not much semantic relation between the new derived word and the two word components.

a. Noun + Verb

1] bu + sun   >   busun   'kitchen'
   rice cook

2] in + leŋ   >   inleŋ   'return'
   house play

3] pǝt + di   >   pǝtdi   'thatch'
   cotton want

4] thǝw + ka   >   thǝwka   'Monday'
   duty   shoot

5] ar + si   >   arsi   'star'
   hen   keep

6] ∂n +   di   >   ∂ndi   'small'
    curry want

7] in +   tuk   >   intuk   'to meet'
    house find

8] kut + si   >   kutsi   'ring'
    hand   keep

b. Noun + Noun

1] tuy + in   >   tuyin   'to drink water'
    water houn

2] wa +   bu   >   wabu   'nest'
    bird   rice

3] in +   ru   >   inru   'to steal'
    house bamboo

4] in +   uy   >   inuy   'laugh'
    house dog

c. Verb + Noun

1] si +   in   >   si-in   'liver'
    keep   house

2] troŋ + th∂y   >   throŋth∂y   'able to speak'
    speak fruit

CHAPTER VI
CLAUSE STRUCTURE

6.1 Simple Sentence

In a simple sentence, there is only one matrix verb; it remarks a simple statement (expressing habitual, natural truth or routin action).

Examples :

1] k∂y bu ki-sak
   I rice 1pp.-eat
   'I eat rice'

2] n∂ŋ bu ni-sak
   'you eat rice'

3] ∂ma bu ∂-sak
   'He eats rice'

The above sentences shows that the language is a verbal prononalized language, that is, for the first person **ki** is prefixed to the verb, **ni** for the second and ∂- for the third person. The preffixes are prefixed to the verbs (see Declarative sentence).

6.2 Complex Sentence

In complex sentence there are two clauses, i.e., one matrix and one or more than two dependent clause, they are connected by the conjunctive particles, namely, **mərəm-wa** 'that' **kən** 'before', **ləya** 'at that time' or 'where' **a** 'after'.

Examples :

4]   kəy ki-rom mərəm-wa kəy-innə intal   thləw
     I   know that   I -nom. mistak work
     'I know that I have made a mistake'

5]   kəy ki-rom   mərəm-wa əma inthə   thleŋ-tu
     I   1pp.know that   he at once come-unreal. asp.
     'I know that he will come at once'

6]   gari-tha se-sa kə-in   stesən kən   tluŋ-no-mə
     bus-det. go-compt. I-noun station before reach-neg.
     'The bus has left before I reached the station'

7]   əma-ləw əm-no-sa   kəy-innə əmə-tiŋ ki-se   ləya
     he-speci/there be-neg.compt. I noun   he dat. 1pp.
     go at that time
     'He is not there when I go to him'

8]   dəktər-in ə-se-nu-a əma   əkjon-mi thleŋ-əy
     doctor-noun 3pp. go compl. after he visit-man
     come-remot.com.mk.
     'The visitors came after the doctor had left'

9]   əma ənətrell əma iskul   se-no
     he ill since he school go-neg.
     'He did not go to school since he is ill'

10] əma kleŋ-lewa kəy iskul se-tuŋ
     he come if   I   school do-unreal.

'If he come I will go to school'

6.3 Compound Sentence

In this type of sentence two or more independent sentences are connected with the help of coordinating conjunction, namely ∂**mace** 'and', **ceyrela** 'therefore', **cuta** 'but' and ∂**macuna** 'so' etc. Examples :-

11] khusur haŋ-sa ∂mace-∂nma inthru suŋ
    rain stop-compt. and they walk out
    'The rain had stopped and they walked out'

12] sinema ce-sa ∂mace kani in-thru suŋ
    film end-compt. and we come out
    'The film has ended and we came out'

13] m∂y mut-sa ∂mace inthru suŋ
    light put off compt. and came out
    'The light has put off and we came out'

14] ∂ma k∂n∂ ceyrela iskul se-no
    he ill therefore school go-neg.
    'He is ill he dinot go to school'

15] ∂ma-i kh∂lmo-a s∂r∂ cuta ∂ril kh∂lmo enrol
    he be poor poor but benevolent great+asp.
    'He is poor but very benevolent'

16] ∂ma tr∂ŋŋa ∂pa ∂macuna n∂mb∂r k∂t∂m ∂ph∂
    he book 3pp. so number very 3pp. get
    'He reads hard so he gets his mark'

In case there are more than two nouns (Tomba, Tombi, John and Jack etc.) in a sentence no connecting or coordinating conjunction is used, only coma is used.

17] tomba, tombi, sila, mona iskul se-ǝy
Tomba, Tombi, Sheela and Mona go to school'

6.4 Conjunction

A conjunction is a joining word which can connect two or more sentences, clauses, phrases and words. It can help in conveying a complete meaning of a construction. In English the words like **and**, **but**, or **therefore**, etc. are conjunct words.

In Tarao, there are a number of words which are used as conjunction. They are the following :

1] le-le   'and'
2] kho-kho   'also'
3] ǝma ǝknu?   'then'
4] ǝmace   'then'
5] mǝrǝmwa   'because'
6] nocele   'or'
7] ǝcuta/ǝmacuta   'even then'
8] cusilakho   'even though'
9] ǝma cunǝ   'therefore'

They are discussed one by one in the followings :

1] Conjunct particle <u>le-le</u> 'and' or 'with'

This conjunction is a suffix which is added to every noun or pronoun occurring in the structure, as in the following examples :

a] tombə-le   cawbə-le   se-tuŋ
   Tomba-conj. Chaoba-conj. go-unreal
   'Tomba and Chaoba will go'

b] kəy-le əma-le   tombə-le   se-tuŋ
   I-conj. he-conj. Tomba-conj. go-unreal.
   'I, he and Tomba will go'

c] əma-le   tombə-le   se-tuŋ
   he-conj. Tomba-conj. go-fut.
   'He goes with Tomba'

2] Conjunct particle <u>kho-kho</u> 'and'

This conjunct particle is added to the noun only like the conjunct particle **le-le**.

d] kipa-kho phadər-kho la   thlo
   my father father   song sing
   'My daddy and father sing song'

3] Conjunct word <u>əma aknu</u> 'then'

e] ca in-ro   əma aknu bu   sak-ro
   tea drink-comd.   then   rice eat-comd.
   'Take tea then rice'

4] Conjunct word ∂mace 'then/and'

It can conjunct phrases and clauses as in the following sentences :

f] n∂ŋ   se-ro   ∂mace   waykh∂t thleŋ-ro
you   go-comd   and/then   again   come-comd.
'You go and (then) come again'
(Today you go I have some works, and come again')

g] ∂m∂kne   se-ro   ∂mace   ∂ma oŋ-ro
there   go-comd   and/then   he   call-comd
'Go there and call him' (Go there and call him to come here)

5] Conjunction m∂r∂mwa 'because'

This conjunction m∂r∂mwa 'because' is used to connect phrase or clauses. Examples are given below.

h] k∂y t∂l sak-no-tuŋ m∂r∂mwa k∂y bu k∂-sak-tuŋ
I roti eat-neg-unreal because I rice 1pp-eat-unreal.
'I will not eat roti because I will take rice'

i] ∂ma k∂ythel-∂ so-no-tuŋ m∂r∂mwa ∂ma larik kh∂t
                                        p∂-tuŋ
he market-loc go-neg-unreal because he book one
                                        read-unreal
'He will not go to market because he will read a book'

6] Conjunction <u>nocele</u> 'either or'

The conjunct word <u>nocele</u> 'either or' can connect words (nouns) or clauses.

 j] tombə nocele cawbə la thlo-ro
   Tomba or Chaoba song sing-comd.
   'Either Tomba or Chaoba sing a song'

 k] nəŋ skul-ə se-ro nocele in-na larik pa-ro
   you school-loc go-comd. or house-loc book read-
                 comd.
   'You go to school or read the book at home.'

7] Conjunction <u>əmacuta/cuta</u> 'even then'

It is used to connect two sentences or clauses.

 l] tombə kədon əmacuta tlen-no
   Tomba rich-emp even then happy-neg.
   'Tomba is rich even then he is not happy'

8] Conjunction <u>cusələkho</u> 'even though'

It is used to join clauses in Tarao.

 m] jon-nə treŋŋə insul cusəlkəho thləwwa kanə-no
   John-nom hard try even though work use-neg.
   'John try very hard even though he fails to do the work'

9] Conjunction <u>əmacunə</u> 'therefore'

It is used to connect sentences in Tarao.

n] jon-nə kəytə ə-kənsleŋ əmacunə kəy sak-no-tuŋ
John-nom. me 3pp-scold therefore I eat-neg-unreal.
"John scolds me, therefore, I will not eat'

CHAPTER VII
SENTENCES PROCESS

7.1 Decalarative sentence

The declarative sentence shows, the verbal pronominalization and shows general word order of the language. Tarao has verbal prominalization. It is shown in the following sentences.

1] kǝy bu   ki-sak
   I   rice 1pp.eat
   'I eat rice'

2] nǝŋ bu ni-sak
   'You eat rice'

3] ǝma bu ǝ-sak
   'He eats rice'

The above prefixes **ki**-in sentence (1) and **ni**-in sentence (2) and ǝ-in sentence (3) are the respective verbal pronominal markers of the respective persons, i.e., first person **key**, second person **nǝŋ** and third person **ǝma**. Verbal pronominalization is only used in Affirmative sentence, only in simple aspect.

It is already said that declarative sentence shows word order of a language. Tarao is a subject-object-verb (SOV) word order. In another word, Tarao is a verb final language. The above three sentences also show it.

a. Numeral follows the noun, as in sentence (4)

4] kəy yukpi khət ki-mu
I   tiger one 1pp.see
'I see a tiger'

b. Adjective follows the noun

5] əma-innə kəy-tiŋŋa rəy kəthra   khət kəmu-əŋ
he-nom. I-accu. flower beautirufl one 1pp-show
'He shows me a nice flower'

c. Determiner follows the noun

6] inru-khə ən sur-pəy
thief det. 3pp.arrest perf.
'The thief is arrested'

d. Adverb procedes the verb

7] əma kəthra-a ə-thlo
he nicely 3pp. sing
'He sings nicely'

8] kəy-ta əmertha uy inŋəw inthum əm
my   nice   dog white three have
'I have three nice white dog'

It also shows that Tarao is a postposition language. The following examples substantiate the statement.

Tarao has case markers which are all suffixed to the noun (see for detail in case).

Tarao has case markers which are all suffixed to the noun (see for detail in case). The locative case markers (∂ and **a**) are suffixed to the words like, **∂pal∂** 'outside', **cuŋ** 'on', **koma** 'near', **insuŋ** 'inside', **thaŋ** 'under'etc. It is a postpositioned language.

9] ∂ma ∂pal∂   inthru-sa
    he outside loc. move out-asp.
    'He goes out'

10] ∂ma insuŋ-ŋa ∂m
    he inside loc. stay
    'He goes inside'

11] ∂wa koma ∂ma   insil
    river near he take bath
    'He takes bath in the bank of the river'

12] layrik teb∂l thaŋ-ŋa ∂m
    book table under loc. stay
    'The book in under the tabel'

7.2 Negation

In Tarao, negation is formed with the suffixation of negative marker -**no** which is followed by a non-future marker -∂ŋ. It (-∂ŋ) indicates a habitual meaning as well as the action occurred in the past (non-future), denying an action happening in the past. The pronominal prefix, such as , **ki-**, **ni-** and ∂- respectively for first person, second person and third person are deleted in the negative formation.

1.a] kəy bu ki-sak
     I   rice 1pp.eat
     'I eat rice'

b]   kəy bu sak-no-əŋ
     'I do not take rice'

2.a] tomba la ə-thlo
     Tomba song 3pp. sing
     'Tomba does sing'

b]   tomba la thlo-no-əŋ
     'Tomba does not sing'

3.a] in-ni tək ə-sak
     they meat 3pp.eat
     'They does not eat meat'

b]   in-ni tək thlo-no-əŋ
     'They does not eat meat'

In future a suffix **-tu** or **tuŋ** is added to the negative marker **-no**. See the following examples.

3]   kipa   dili   se-no-tu
     my father Delhi go neg-unreal.
     'My father will not go to Delhi'

5]   tomba la   thlo-no-tu
     Tomba song sing neg-unreal.

'Tomba will not sing'

6] kɘy sinema ɘn-no-tuη
   I   cinema see neg-unreal.
   'I will not see the picture'

The future marker -**tuη** is used with the first person pronoun in negation while -**tu** occurs elsewhere.

7.2.1 Prohibitive

In Tarao, prohibitive is formed by suffixation of negative marker -**no** followed by the command marker -**ro**, as in the following sentences.

7.a] pa-ro
      read-comd.mk.

  b] pa-no-ro
      'Don't read'

8.a] se-no
      go -comd.mk.
      'Go'

  b] se-no-ro
      'Don't go'

9.a] kani in-nɘ   thleη-ro
      our house-loc. come-comd.mk.
      'Come to hour house'

b]   kani in-n∂ thleŋ-no-ro
      'Don't come to our house'

7.2.2 Double negation

In the construction of double negation in Tarao, a word
k∂no is used along with non-future marker -∂ŋ occurring
finally in the sentence.

10]   k∂y m∂kha ya-no   k∂no-∂ŋ
       I   that agree-neg. d.neg.non.fut.
       'It is not that I disagree to that'

11]   k∂y la-kha   th∂y-no   k∂no-∂ŋ
       I   song-det. listen-neg. d.neg.non.fut.
       'It is not that I did not listen to that song'

12]   ∂ma sak-no   k∂no-∂ŋ
       he eat-neg. d.neg. non.fut.
       'It is not that I did not eat'

13]   k∂ni se-no   k∂no-∂ŋ
       we go-neg. d.neg. non.fut.
       'It is not that we did not go'

It is learnt that in double negation a word **k∂no** along
with a non-future marker -∂ŋ is used in addition to the
negative marker -**no** which is suffixed to the main verb.

7.2.3 Negative strengthening

In most of the languages, negative is strengthened with
an additional word, such as **never**, **at all** in English. In

Tarao it is strengthened by a word **luŋ** which follows the verb plus negative marker (V+no).

14] əma loy-no   luŋ
      he say-neg never
      'He never say'

15] əma kələm-kha ləw-no   luŋ
      he pen-det.   take-neg. never
      'He does not take the pen at all'

16] ənma dili   se-no luŋ
      they Delhi go-neg. never
      'They never go to Delhi'

17] əma leŋ-no   luŋ
      he play-neg. never
      'He never play'

18] tomba yuy   in-no   luŋ
      Tomba liquor drink-neg. never
      'Tomba never drinks liquor'

From the above sentences it is learnt that negative is strengthened by the word **luŋ**. On the whole, the word **luŋ** emphasised the negative meaning.

7.3 Imperative

Imperative expresses command, request and proposal.

7.3.1 Command

Command in this language is constructed by the suffixation of the morphemes -ro for singular and -we for plural to the main verb. Generally, in this language, subject is understood.

Command marker -ro :

1] wa - ro
    come-comd.mk.
    'Come'

2] dili   se-ro
    Delhi go-comd.mk.
    'Go to Delhi'

3] tuy   gilas khət thlem-ro
    water glass one bring-comd.mk.
    'Bring a glass of water'

The understood subject in these sentences are in singular number, i.e., -ro is used in singular number.

Command marker -we:

4] tək sak-we
    meat eat-comd.mk.
    'You (pl.) eat meat'

5] ca   in-we
    tea drink-comd.mk.
    'You (pl.) drink tea'

7.3.2 Request

It is formed by suffixing a request marker -**man** followed by the command marker -**ro** (sg.) and -**we** (pl.) to the verb.

6] pa-man-ro
   read req. comd.mk.
   'Please read' (sing.)

7] maji-man-we
   write req. comd.mk.(pl.)
   'Pleace write'

There are other types of imerative, namely, permission imperative, conditional imperative, 'Let' imperative. They are discussed shortly in the followings.

7.3.3 Permission imperative

In its formation, there is no other additional morpheme, only the command suffix -**ro** is added to the verbal root.

8] ma-i-thra   nəη-nə   nikdit pot-kha   ləy-ro
   it be good you-nom. like   thing-det. buy-comd.mk.
   'It is good, buy whatever you want'

9] ma-i-kituy   nəη-nə   sa-ya   pot-kha   sa-ro
   it be tasty you-nom. eat-choose thing-det. eat-
                                                comd.mk.
   'It is tasty, eat whatever you want'

10] nilǝy-ya   pot-tal-kha lǝy-ro
      buy choose   thing-det.   buy-comd.mk.
      'Buy whatever you want to buy'

7.3.4 Conditional imperative

It is also constructed through the suffixation of the command marker -**ro** to the verbal root; no other additonal morpheme is added, in the construction only a pause or a coma is used, as in the following sentences.

11] kani in-nǝ   thleη-ro,   kǝy-nǝ pǝysa ki-pek-tu
      our house-loc. come-comd. I-nom.   money Ipp.
                                                    give fut.mk.
      'Come to our house, I will give you money'

7.4.5 'Let' imperative

Construction of 'let' imperative in Tarao is completed in the sense that there are different morphemes for inclusive and exclusive speaker, more and above, a different morpheme is used for the first person and another morpheme for the third person.

a. For 'let' for the first person singular, the command marker -**ro** is suffixed to the verb, at the same time a proposal word **kǝm** is prefixed to the verb and the accusative marker -**tǝ** is suffixed to the first personal pronoun **kǝy** 'I'.

12] kǝy-tǝ kǝm-leη-ro
      I-accu. pro. play-comd.mk.
      'Let me play'

b. 'Let' for the third person plural a proposal marker **-r∂y**
   is suffixed to the verb.

14] ∂n-ma m∂-se-r∂y
   they   3pp. go-pro.mk.
   'Let them go'

15] ∂n-ma m∂-th∂y-r∂y
   they   3pp. teach pro.mk.
   'Let them teach'

c. 'Let' inclusive speaker

If the speaker is included, the 'let' marker is **-rase**
which is added to the verb.

16] in-ma   tlo-rase
   we-incl. do-pro.mk.
   'Let's do this'

17] in-ma   se-rase
   we include. go-pro.mk.
   'Let's us go'

d. 'Let' imperative with third person

It is formed by the suffixation **-seso** to the verbal root.

18] ∂ma se-seso
   he   go-pro.mk.
   'Let him go'

7.3.6 'Let' request

It is formed by the suffixation of the marker **-risa** to the verbal root, at the same time a proposal word **kəm** is used in the construction. It is interesting that these linguistic entity **kəm** and the suffix -risa are used with the first proposal pronoun (Singular), as in the sentence (19).

19] kəy-tə kəm se-risa
I -acc. pro. go-req.mk.
'Let me go please'

7.4 Interrogative

There are generally two major types of questions. One is Yes/No question another is Inquiry questions, generally known as wh-question.

7.4.1 Yes/No question

The formation of Yes/No question is different from other TB languages, like Manipuri, Thadou, Paite etc., in which the question marker is simply suffixed to the verb. But in the case of Yes/No question in Tarao, one of the auxialiary verbs, namely **cek** 'can' or **ce** 'do' or **pəy** 'have/has' is needed. And the question marker -**me** is added to the auxialiary verb, at the same time the pronominal marker, ə- third person marker and **ni**- second person marker, is prefixed to the auxiliary verb. Thus Yes/No question in Tarao is constructed.

1] nəŋ iŋlis troŋ ni-cek-me
you English speak 2pp. can-q.mk.

'Can you speak English?'

2] naw   bu   sak   ∂-cek-me
child rice   eat   3pp. can q.mk.
'Can the child eat rice ?'

3] la   thlok ni-cek-me
song   sing   2pp. can q.mk.
'Can you sing ?'

4] n∂ŋ   bu   sak   ni-p∂y-me
you   rice   eat   2pp. aux.q.mk.
'You taken your meal ?'

The question marker -**me** can be added to noun also in the equative sentence but it cannot function as a verb 'be'. A different morpheme -**i** functions as a verb 'be' and it (-**i**) is added to the pronoun, as in sentence (5) and (6).

5] ∂ma-i jon-me
he-be john-q.mk.
'Is he John?'

6] ∂ma-i dokt∂r-me
he-be doctor-q.mk.
'Is he a doctor ?'

7.4.2 Wh-question

In Tarao, wh-question is formed with a question word and a question marker -**me** is added to the verb. The question words in this language are like, **nirkh/tu-in** 'who', **y∂ŋ-** 'what', **y∂k** 'which', **y∂ŋrela** 'why', **y∂ŋnuŋ** 'when' and **rəm-ma** 'where'. It can be noted that the question marker -**me** can be added to the question word and it gives respective question, as in the followings :

1. mətha-me 'who' ? (who is)

2. yəŋ-me 'what' ? (what is this)

3. yək-me 'which' ? (which is)

4. yəŋrela-me 'why' ? (why is)

5. yəŋnuŋ-me 'when' ? (when will)

6. rəm-ma-me 'where' ? (where is)

Besides these short questions, in other wh-questions the question marker -**me** is suffixed to the verb and the auxiliary verb, like **cek** 'can', **ce** 'do' and **pəy** 'have/has' do not occur in the construction.

7] tu-in əmjom-me
   who help-q.mk.
   'Who helps you?'

8] əma yəŋ əthlok-me
   he what 3pp.do-q.mk.
   'Who is doing ?'

9] yəŋ ni-thlen-me
   what 2pp. bring-q.mk.
   'Waht do you bring here ?'

10] yak nəŋ luŋlut ni-dit-me
    which you shirt 2pp. liki-q.mk.
    'Which shirt do you like ?'

11] layrik-ə khəthoə   ni-khut-me
    book   that how   2pp. get-q.mk.
    'How do you get that book ?'

12] khəthoə ni-rəl-me
    how   2pp. cross-q.mk.
    'How does he cross ?'

13] yəŋrela   ni-mla-me
    why   2pp. leave-q.mk.
    'Why does he leave ?'

14] əma yəŋnuŋ   ə-thleŋ-me
    he when   3pp. return-q.mk.
    'When does he return ?'

7.4.3 Alternative question

In Tarao, alternative questions can be constructed in three various ways. (a) Verb alternative, (b) Noun allernative and (c) by using a connective word **cunole** 'either or'. They are discussed below :

a. Verb alternative

It is formed by the suffixation of -**uce** to the verb just before the question marker -**me**. In this alternative question, there are two verb phrases positive VP and negative VP (negative marker suffixed VP). The positive VP precedes the negative VP : this order is rigid.

15] nəŋ deli-ya   nise-uce-me ni-se-no-uce me
    you Delhi-loc. go-alt.q.mk.   go-neg. alt. q.mk.
    'Whether will you go to Delhi or not ?'

16a] nəŋ tək   ni-sak-uce-me,   ni-sak-uce-me
    you meat 2pp. eat-alt.-q.mk. 2pp. eat-alt.-q.mk.
    'Whether will you eat meat or not ?'

b]   əma skul   se-uce-me   se-no-uce-me
      he   school go-alt.-q.mk. go-neg. alt. q.mk.
      'Whether he goes to school or not ?'

c]   əma layrik-kha ləy-uce-me ly-no-umeme
      'Whether he buys the book or not ?'

b. Noun alternative

In the construction of alternative question of nouns (either or of two nouns) a suffix -**ume** is added to two verbs. There is no question of negative morpheme in this construction. Another morpheme of alternative marker -**nun** is suffixed to the nouns, as in sentences (17).

17]   ca-num in ume   səŋgom-num in-ume
      tea alt. drink-alt.q.mk. milk-alt.   drink-alt.q.mk.
      'Do you drink tea or milk'

c. Use of connective words cunole 'either or'

In this type alternative question construction, a conective word **cunole** 'either or' is used as well as the question marker -**me** is suffixed to the noun or to the verb.

18]   əma əmji-i nəŋ-cime cunole əma-me
      he   writer-be you det.q.mk. or he-q.mk.
      'Whether the writer is he or you?'

19] nƏŋ tƏk   mi-sak-cime   cunole bu   ni-sak-ci-me
you meat 2pp.-eat det.q.mk. or rice 2pp. eat. det.
q.mk.

'Whether you eat meat or rice ?'

7.4.4 Tag question

In Tarao, tag question is formed by suffixation of -**rƏyme** to the verb in the positive tag question while in the negative tag, the negative marker -**no** is added before -**rƏyme**. Tarao has only reversed tag question.

20a] sila   Əsək thra, thra-no-rƏy-me
Sheela face nice, nice-neg.-tag.-q.mk.
'Sheela is nice is not it ?'

20b] sila Əsək thipƏ, thi-no-rƏy-me
'Sheela is ugly, is not it ?'

21a] Əma bu sa-no,   sa-rƏy-me
he rice eat-neg., eat-tag-q.mk.
'He does not eat rice, is it ?'

21b] Əma tƏk Əsək, sa-no-rƏy-me
'He eat meat, is not it ?'

22a] nƏŋ taraw ce, ce-no-rƏy-me
you Tarao be, be-neg.-tag-q.mk.
'You are Tarao, aren't you ?'

22b] nƏŋ taraw ce-no,   ce-rƏy-me
'You are not Tarao, is it ?'

Tag question in imperative

23a] tuy gilas thlen-ro, thlen-no-r∂y-me
water glass bring-comd. bring-neg.-tag-q.mk.
'Bring a glass of water, won't you ?'

23b] tuy gilas thlen-no-ro, thlen-r∂y-me
'Don't bring a glass of water, will you ?'

7.5 Optative Sentence

It expresses wishes and it is formed through the suffixation -**so** to the verbal root.

1] isor-n∂   k∂l-so
god-nom. save opt.mk.
'God may save him'

2] ∂ma punsi-so
he   long-live-opt.mk.
'May he live long'

3] ∂ma thlen-n∂   ∂m-so
he   happy-adv. live -opt.mk.
'May he live happily'

7.6 Exclamatory sentence

Excamatory expresses the sudden feelings and emotions of happiness and sorrow. For the expression of sudden emotion, a phrase **ale luŋ sa** 'alas' is used in the begining of the sentence.

1] ale-luŋ-sa ∂ma ∂pa thisa
   alas   he   his father dead
   'Alas ! his father is dead !'

2] ale-luŋ-sa n∂w thisa
   alas   child dead
   'Alas ! the child is dead !'

Unlike the expression of sorrow, in the expression of happiness the very phrase, **ale-luŋ-sa** is not used. It is expressed with the high inotonation of utterance.

3] k∂ni k∂n-thoy-p∂y
   we 1pp. win-asp.
   'We have won the match'

A particular word **uk-a** is also used in exclamatory to express the emotional feelings when one is attracted with surprise.

4] pol-e uk-a ∂thra-sa
   how excl. nice-
   'How wonderful is this !'

And ∂s can be added as apposition to express a surprise mood with **uk-a**.

5] ∂s la-co uk-a ∂thra-sa
   excl. song-det. excl. nice
   'How nice is this song !'

CHAPTER VIII
FORMS OF ADDRESS

Forms of address are closely related to social structure as well as inter personal relationships between the addressee and speaker.

a. Kinship terms of address

The modes of address used by Tarao community are closely related to kinship terms. In Tarao community limited kinship terms are used for different kinship relations.

∂nu	'my mother'
∂pa	'my father'
pate	'aunt'
nute	'sister (e)'
ute	'brother (e)'
hunpi	'sister-in-law (male ego)
m∂n	'sister-in-law (female ego)
thrur	'brother-in-law (male ego)
hanch∂	'brother-in-law (female ego)
ni	'mother-in-law'
m∂r∂ŋ	'father-in-law'

Address by name

Usual and most common form of address is to call a person by his or her name. if a person's name is 'Ramu' the elders in his family address him by his name.

In Tarao, the wife do not call her husband by name, instead of it a displace word **uythƏy-me** 'are you listening' is used; or she can used her son's or daughter's name like **Mo**-pa or **Te**-pa (pa 'father').

Naming system

Tarao has a culture of naming their sons or daughters according to order.

a. Son

The first son is named as 'Mo'
The second son is named as 'Ko'
The third son is named as 'Me'

b. Daughter

The first daughter is named as 'Te'
The second daughter is named as 'To'
The third daughter is named as 'sƏŋ'

APPENDIX I

Some word can have different meanings in this language as in the following examples :

1] ∂n   'look'
    ∂n   'curry'

2] in   'drink'
    ⁱn   'sleep'
    in   'house'

3] thi   'die'
    thi   'ginger'

4] ci   'salt'
    ci   'end'

5] ka   'room'
    ka   'shoot'

6] la   'thred'
    la   'song'

7] ni   'day'
    ni   'pronominal prefix'
    ni   'two'

8] ∂ya   'permission'
    ∂ya   'way' possibility
    ∂ya   'oh' (mood of excitement)

9] əm 'have'
əm 'live'

10] rəy 'flower'
rəy 'ax'
rəy 'aspect mk.'

11] suŋ 'in or inside'
suŋ 'pour'

12] mu 'sow'
mu 'lip'
mu 'see'

13] som 'squeze'
som 'ten'

14] ce 'end'
ce 'paper'

15] əkni 'behind'
əkni 'bake'

I. Like wise the prefis **ki-, ni** and ə- can be used as a subjunctive pronoun or a nominative pronoun in the following examples :

1] ki - way laya 'I was'
ni- way laya 'you were'
ə - way laya 'she/he was'

II. Usually the pronominal prefix ə- indicates 3rd person singular number when it is prefixed to a (verbal), but to the noun it has no meaning. Examples :

1] əwa   'river'

    ə + wa   'bird'

So in the above example the second syllable of the word (**əwa**) /wa/ means 'bird' whereas the first syllable /ə/ becomes meaningless.

A word can be analysed into two or more parts giving a meaningful unit of each part as in the following examples :

1] kipa   <   ki   +   pa   'my father'

                pro.pre. father

2] nipa   <   ni   +   pa   'you father'

                pro.pre father

3] əpa   <   ə   +   pa   'his/her father'

                pro.pre. father

The first syllable of these three words **ki-**, **ni-** and **ə-** are derived from the 1st person **kəy** 'I' , 2nd person **nəŋ** 'you' and **əma** 'he/her' respectively. They have also possessive meaning like 'my', 'your' and 'his/her' etc.

Contrary to above **ni-** is not always used as a pronominal prefix but it can be used as a noun, as a verb in infinitive. Examples :

As a noun

1]	nikhət	<	ni + khət		'one day'
			day	one	

As a verb

2]	nisak	<	ni + sak		'to eat'
			to	eat	
3]	nilon	<	ni + lon		'to throw'
			to	throw	
4]	niin	<	ni + in		'to drink'
			to	drink	

III. -**ni** becomes meaningless when it is added at the end of certain words.

Examples :

1]	əkni	<	ək + ni		'behind'
2]	əkni	<	ək + ni		'bake'

IV. **ək-** becomes a meaningful part when it is used in stative verbs and is used for the formation of adjective in contrast to above examples.

1]	əkday	<	ək + day		'to be cold'
2]	əkdi	<	ək + di		'to be small'
3]	əkthra	<	ək + thra		'to be nice'

V. The component of a compound word have a meaning of its own.

Examples:

1] əknu   <   ək   +   nu   'after'
                  actor noun mother

2] əkthra   <   ək   +   thra 'a nice person or
                  actor nou nice   thing'

3] əkcek   <   ək   +   cek   'can or be able'
                  actor noun can

Morphemes which can be analysed into two parts. Either part can have a meaning of its own. On the other hand it ca be called as compounding. Examples :

1] inni   <   in + ni   'we'
                house day or sun

2] yəŋnəŋ   <   yəŋ + nəŋ   'which'
                what   you

3] mitmul   <   mit + mul   'eye lash'
                eye   body hair

4] silek   <   sil + ek   'cow dung'
                cow   dung

5] seŋno   <   seŋ + no   'blue'
                clear vegetable marker

6] bular   <   bu + lar   'famine'
                   rice dry

7] thirnu   <   thir + nu   'magnate'
                   iron mother

8] kutsi   <   kut + si   'ring'
                   hand keep

9] somŋa   <   som + ŋa   'fifty'
                   ten   so

10] wabu   <   wa + bu   'nest'
                   bird cooked rice

11] saru   <   sa + ru   'bone'
                   child bamboo

12] inru   <   in + ru   'steal'
                   drink bamboo

Some Compound words

1] cesa   <   ce + sa   'finish'
                   end go

2] rusun   <   ru +   sun   'root of a
                   bamboo cook   plant'

3] busun   <   bu + sun   'kitchen'
                   rice cook

4] innəw   <   in + nəw   'fat'
                   drink brother(y)

5] əkseŋ   <   ək + seŋ   'fresh'
                 act. no. clear

6] inleŋ   <   in + leŋ   'return'
                 drink play

7] inru   <   in + ru   'theif'
                 house bamboo

8] inleŋ   <   in + leŋ   'losse'
                 house play

9] incuŋ   <   in + cuŋ   'vibrate'
                 house on or above

10] səkolcuŋ <   səkol + cuŋ   'ridding'
                 horse   on or above

11] troŋthəyno < troŋ + thəy + no   'dumb'
                 speak fruit   a negative marker

Having meaning of the 1st part only

1]   uytrok   <   uy + trok   'dog'
                 dog   meaningless

trok- the second part is meaningless

2]   inpal   <   in + pal   'floor'
                 house meaningless

3]   əndon   <   ən + don   'hope'
                 curry meaningless

4] thiŋbur < thiŋ + bur 'leaves'
tree meaningless

5] iŋkhar < iŋ + khar 'door'
meaningless sheet

6] luŋlut < luŋ + lut 'shirt'
stone meaningless

7] kejuŋ < ke + juŋ 'to fly'
leg meaningless

APPENDIX II

Vocabulary

Common animals

animal	sa
cow	or
bull	silc∂l
bear	kuw∂m
buffalo	silloy
cat	tuŋkh∂n
calf	silte
camel	ur
dog	uy
dear	saki
elephant	kusay
goat	hameŋ
horse	sakol
lion	noŋsa
monkey	yoŋ
pig	wok
fox	r∂muy
tiger	yokpi
wild pig	buŋ∂l
wild cow	sirim
rat	muju
puppy	uyte

Common birds

bird	wa
bat	bak

cock	arkhoŋ
crow	uyak
chicken	arte
duck	ŋanu
hawk	kewar (bərmu)
hen	arpuy
owl	uybək
pickock	wahoŋ
pigeon	ukthru
parrot	tenəwa
sparrow	usək
sparrow	phəkle
vulture	laŋtia

Common fruits

fruit	thəy
appricot	ləymathəy
apple	thəytup
banana	mot
berry	sumarek
coconut	yubi
cucumber	thopi
date palm	khantup
grapes	aŋkur
gauva	tolthəy
jack fruit	thəypom
lemon	cəmpra
mango	həynəw
orange	komla
papaya	busen
pomegranate	kəpoy
pear	suphaythetuk
tamarind	məŋgithəy

Common insects

bug	riksat
butterfly	phalep
cockroach	khƏlaw
dragonfly	saŋteŋ
fly	muthu
garden lizard	aykin
grass hopper	khaw
honey bee	khuy
insect	cirik
leech	tilpa
snail	morwat
spider	imuŋmƏraŋ
quark	khƏroy
wall lizard	thransa

Vegetables

bean	be
brinjal	bƏtcho
cabbage	kopi
cauliflower	kopilƏy
garlic	tƏklƏw
gourd	khoŋtum
ginger	thi
green chilli	morok siriŋ
ladies finger	sƏmnal
mustard	Əntrum
oxalis	arsukma
onion	piƏs
pea	bithu
pepper	moroksi
potato	Əlu
pumpkin	may

sweet potato	mə̄ŋkara
sugar cane	mə̄su
soyabean	bethru

Name of the days

day	ni
sun	ni
Sunday	noŋmayciŋ
Monday	thə̄wka
Tuesday	pə̄pok
Wednusday	sə̄ysa
Thusday	sə̄kolsel
Friday	iray
Saturday	thaŋca
today	ini-in
yesterday	mə̄yan
tomorrow	tuŋwa
day before yesterday	di-in
day after tomorrow	tuyba
month	thla
year	kum
next	mə̄thə̄ŋ
next month	mə̄thə̄ŋ thla
last month	ə̄ksece thla
last	ə̄ksece
last year	ə̄kseche kum
next year	mə̄thə̄ŋ kum

Kinship terms and forms of address

father	pa
mother	nu
brother (e)	u
brother (y)	nə̄w

sister (e)	ute
sister (y)	nute
father's brother(y)	panaw
father's brother(e)	h∂nca
mother's sister(e)	nupi
mother's sister(y)	nute
mother-in-laws	ni
father-in-laws	m∂r∂ŋ
cousin (brother)	p∂te
cousin (sister)	nute
sister-in-laws	m∂w
aunt	nu
man	makupa
woman	kum∂y
child	naw
children	naw-miyam
boy	pate
girl	pite

Common disease

diarrhoea	kluŋ
blind	mitco
deaf	kurp∂ŋ
dump	troŋth∂yno
lame	∂ke klik
handicap	s∂wrel
leprocy	r∂yci
diabetes	yuŋtruŋ
indigestion	w∂n nuŋsitka
swelling	thluŋsuk
tablet	l∂yeŋ
nurse	n∂rs
hospital	d∂kt∂rs∂ŋ

local physician	maypa
mid wife	maypi

Common goods of everyday use

almirah	apu
air	khilraŋ
bucket	beltin
bed	kukthol
box	upu
cloth	punsil
chair	cəwki
cigarette	brina
chicken	arte
ax	rəy
bred	təl
beaf	silkor
book	layrik
dagger	cəmpa
door	iŋkhar
egg	ərtuy
fire-wood	thiŋ
flesh	kor
fire	məy
glass	cəpla
grass	dəw
gun	rukməy
frying pan	khaŋ
knife	cem
light	məy
lantern	lartiŋ
looking glass	bəjəŋ
milk	silcu
meat	tək

mosquito net	kh∂l
pen	kolom
pencil	pensil
paper	ce
plate	pukh∂m
pot	belthuη
pellar	kokko
pork	kor
rice	busay
cooked rice	bu
roof	incuη
quilt	punmuthu
pillow cover	mokhum
pillow	mokh∂n
spear	kuksay
song	la
spoon	khroy
shocks	moca
shirt	lut
thatch	b∂tir
tea	ca
tea leaf	cana
table	teb∂l
water	tuy
wool	ul
wall	b∂η
key	co
hill	mul
river	∂wa
pond	pukhri
tree	thiη
dry	car
sky	kuwar

wel	cor
east	noŋpok
west	noŋcup
south	kha
north	∂waŋ
colour	m∂cu
white	ŋ∂w
black	w∂m
red	∂ŋ
skyblue	∂duŋ
yellow	∂naw

Pronouns

I	k∂y
we	k∂yni
you	n∂ŋ
you (pl)	nini
he	∂ma
they	∂nma
me	k∂yta
my	k∂y
your	n∂ŋta
his	∂m∂ta
her	∂m∂ta
him	∂ma
their	∂nmata
them	∂nma
our	kinita

Wh- question words

who	tun∂ŋ
what	y∂ŋ

which	y∂η n∂η
where	r∂mma
when	y∂nn∂η
how	y∂ηn∂ηa
why	y∂ηrela

Part of the body

armpit	lkya
bear	m∂khamul
brain	ben
belly	w∂n
breast	lukhe
body hair	mul
blood	thi
bone	saru
buttock	niη
cheech	ikbiη
chest	lukhe/om
chin	imkha
eye	mit
eye lash	mitmul
elbow	kil
eye-brow	mitn∂rmul
forehead	imc∂l
ear(s)	na
gold finger	kutjom
heel	kemathoη
hip	khlukhethuy
hand	kut
head	h∂η
hair	s∂m
gum	inti
intestive	iril

joints	∂kcaŋ
knee	ikhuk
lip	mu
leg	ke
liver	liver
mouth	baw
moustache	khamul
nose	na
nerve	siŋli
nail	m∂si
navel	imlay
palm	kutm∂ya
stomach	ewonpi
shoulder	edar
thump	kutpi
toe (s)	kepi
teeth	ha
back bone	koŋru
tongue	iml∂y
throat	iturn∂ŋ
skin	ibuŋ
wrist	kutriŋ
waist	emnak
face	may
neck	rukiŋ
chest	om
elbow	kil
body	n∂kcaŋ

Dictionary words

able	∂kcek
accuse	∂mral
ache	k∂na

admit	∂yap∂y
again	enleŋ
after	∂knu
age	kum
air	khliraŋ
all	∂mam
alone	kikru
also	makho
always	∂namte
anger	k∂saw
answer	m∂s∂ŋ
appetite	w∂ntram
appoint	kh∂l
arrive	thuŋ
arrow	tholse
ash	m∂ywut
ask	ruy
bad	thrano
bake	∂kni
bald	k∂ŋtleŋ
ban	khar
bark	indram
beak	∂km∂y
beat	khon
before	∂ma
below	∂thl∂ŋ
between	∂kar
big	∂nrol
bind	kar
bite	∂y
bitter	inkha
blind	mico
blow	yak

blunt	mukul
blur	seŋno
boat	mᴧli
boil	phul
bow	thᴧl
box	upu
boy	nᴧw
bracelet	kolcᴧw
branch	ᴧbak
break	koy
breath	phuk
brick	khioŋ
bright	inkle
bud	inmom
burn	kaŋ
busy	thᴧwcil
bottle	likli
calculate	ᴧŋkᴧ
calm	ᴧkday
cold	kᴧday
care	ceksilro
carry	khlenro
catch	mᴧŋ (sur)
chance	inlen
charm	khathra
chase	thrur
cheap	noŋ
child	naw
choice	ᴧkcᴧr
begin	ᴧhᴧw
clay	philcop
clear	seŋ
climb	kᴧl

cloud	sumphay
collide	incuk
colour	əmcu
combine	intrim
come	khleŋ
consider	intel
console	mənem
conspire	inruŋ
continue	etlokno
cottage	thlam
country	tukləy
courage	kənthithra
coward	kənthithrano
crab	brina
cow shed	silun
curry	ən
cow dung	silek
current	icel
cradle	thoy
cruel	kusar
certain	khəmcuŋ
cut	təŋ
dagger	patham (təksi)
damage	kəmaŋ
dance	lam
danger	waysi
dark	thin
down	niwardi
decide	nir
delay	puno
demand	əkni
dense	incam
depend	mikhapol

desert (v)	mǝtha
die	thi
difficult	kulu
claw	ǝmsin
dig	cǝw
dirty	kǝnǝ
disease	kǝla
distance	insem
divide	inthek
divorce	thlo
do	inkhar
door	mǝŋ
dream	mǝŋ
dress	punrǝy
drink	(tuy-)in
drive	ǝkthopǝy
dust	bur
duty	thǝw
eager	kǝral
eat	sak
elder	unpa
end	ce
enemy	injek
enough	mǝtik
earth	prithibi
enter	ǝsoŋ
equal	intrim
escape	inlit
event	inlaw
evil	thrano
express	ǝmduŋ
extinguist	inthlud
fail	insoy

fall	k∂thla
famine	bucar
far	inn∂w
fear	k∂thrano
feed	thun-∂ms∂k
field	incun
fight	inkhon
find	tuk
finish	cesa
flame	intruη
flat	intlap
float	∂leyu
floor	inpal
fly	ηuη
fog	inbum
fold	m∂thlaph
fool	k∂p∂η
food	saphu
fort	imd∂nn∂
freeze	k∂day
fresh	∂kseη
friend	m∂lsa
frog	uytrok
fun	∂sim
future	∂knu
game	leη
garden	iηkhol
gate	thoηkal
gentle	∂kcim
gift	inpe
girl	kum∂y
give	∂kpe

glad	romthok
go	se
god	∂kpu
gold	s∂na
good	∂kthra
grave	rusun
great	∂nrol
group	grup
habit	∂th∂yna
half	t∂ŋkhay
hammer	sek
hang	m∂thoy
hard	∂sek
harm	k∂j∂w
hate	inter
health	∂kthra
hear	ruŋay
heat	kulum
heavy	kirik
here	m∂kh∂n
hide	m∂thup
hit	m∂troŋ
hoise	n∂nkay
hole	∂khur
home	in
honest	∂rilseŋ
hope	∂ndon
horn	∂ki
hot	∂nsa
hour	puŋ
hurt	s∂yhay
ice	hur

idle	t∂l
ill	k∂na
image	nim
incline	inbay
infinite	inroml∂w
inquire	∂krul
insult	injukpe
invent	∂mthru
iron	thir
island	khuŋloy
it	∂kiŋ
jar	bel
jealous	inn∂r
journey	loy
juice	∂tuy
jump	k∂coŋ
jute	toŋpruy
keep	si
kick	kaw
kill	th∂t
king	kuruŋ
kiss	k∂co
kite	tel∂ŋga
know	∂rom
ladder	setrum
laddle	pukhe
lap	l∂k
large	∂nrol
last	∂kce
late	thil
laugh	inuy
leaf (n)	thiŋbur
leak	inho

learn	∂ktum
left	∂mthr∂
length	∂ks∂y
life	punsi
like	∂kdi
line	l∂m
liquid	∂tul
liquor	tuyba
little	∂ndi
look	∂n
loose	inleŋ
love	rilwol
low	in-nim
mad	inna
magnate	thirnu
make	∂ksem
man	kupa
marriage	c∂ŋwaŋ
mat	phar
meal	m∂rupsa
medicine	ay
meet	intuk
melt	in-noy
modest	insem
mole	s∂mon
morning	yukyiŋ
moon	thla
mother	nu
mourn	tinta
mud	philcop
multiply	puriba
nest	wabu
net	caŋ

new	∂kth∂r
news	paw
next	∂knur
nice	∂kthra
night	khul∂w
noise	olaŋ
now	epek
oath	troŋnir
ocean	s∂mudra
old	∂kth∂r
on	∂cuŋ
open	m∂hoŋ
oppose	inluŋ
origin	inthrukna
ornament	intiŋ
other	∂kthl∂y
paddy	saŋ
page	lamay
pair	∂kl∂ŋ
paper	ce
pet	won
picture	photo
piece	∂kir
place	∂ph∂m
play	leŋ
plenty	nuyl∂ŋ
poor	inr∂n
pour	suŋ
praise	m∂thl∂
prepare	insem
prize	m∂na
proud	k∂thoy

pull	inkay
pure	∂kseŋ
put	∂ksi
quench	thra
quite	∂kcik
race	l∂mel
rain	khu
read	pa
reap	s∂nwat
reduce	imleŋ
rest	inŋay
return	inleŋ
rich	kudol
river	∂wa
riddle	s∂kolcuŋ
ride	thouba
right	c∂ŋ
ring	kutsi
right (correct)	∂kcim
ripe	min
rise	inth∂w
road	l∂m
rock	mul
roof	thiŋwuŋ
room	ka
rotten	∂kṭhu
round	∂koy
rub	∂knal
run	tlan
rush	incun
roap	ruy
root	rutuy
rainy season	sunray

sale	kə-əlt
saline	kaŋo
save	lənyom
sow	mu
say	troŋsən
scold	sal
score	incal
seed	əmu
seek	əkten
seleek	əkcar
send	əkca
shadow	nim
shame	injuk
share	cum
sharp	ya-ik
shoot	ka
show	mənu
shut	khar
set	inbok
sleep	in
slow	təp
small	əndi
smell	əmbrim
smile	nuythrim
smoke	mucup
sneeze	inthi
snow	nur
so	ŋa
soap	cəkpol
soft	ənem
sail	ləyhaw
soldier	ralmi
solid	əphəŋ

some	sǝkte
song	thlo
soon	intha
sorrow	ǝkla
sound	ǝhǝw
soup	ǝtuy
source	ǝhǝwna
spade	ǝkhum
speak	troŋ
spend	mǝmaŋ
spit (v)	mǝcil
spoil	ǝkmaŋ
spoon	khroy
spread	mǝthraw
squeeze	som
stand	nir
starve	carahel
steal	inru
steam	ǝhu
sword	comte
shield	jopak
spear	kuksay
shop	dukan
star	ǝrsi
sky	kuyar
summer	kalentha
sun	ni
sugar	sumyaknǝw
salt	mǝci
wake	ǝyak
walk	se
want	kikdit
warm	kulum

wash	cam
wave	tuym∂l
wax	khoylu
wealth	l∂lthum
wet	cor
wheat	kihu
wheel	c∂ka
wide	∂ntak
win	∂kthloy
wing	∂mthla
witch	soytan
word	lroŋ
write	m∂yji
wrong	∂klay
year	kum
yes	oy
young	inthl∂ŋ
youth	n∂w
zoo	sayok

Numeral Number

one	kh∂t
two	ni
three	thum
four	m∂li
five	raŋa
six	kuruk
seven	siri
eight	kirit
nine	ku
ten	som
eleven	soml∂y kh∂t
twelve	soml∂y ni

thirteen	soml∂y thum
fourteen	soml∂y m∂li
fifteen	soml∂y raŋa
sixteen	soml∂y l∂y kuruk
seventeen	soml∂y siri
eighteen	soml∂y kirit
nineteen	soml∂y ku
twenty	somni
twenty one	somnil∂y kh∂t
twenty two	somnil∂y ni
twenty three	somnil∂y thum
twenty four	somnil∂y m∂li
twenty five	somnil∂y raŋa
twenty six	somnil∂y kuruk
twenty seven	somnil∂y siri
twenty eight	somnil∂y kirit
twenty nine	somnil∂y ku
thirty	somthum
thirty one	somthuml∂y kh∂t
thirty two	somthuml∂y ni
thirty three	somthuml∂y thum
thirty four	somthuml∂y m∂li
thirty five	somthuml∂y raŋa
thirty six	somthuml∂y kuruk
thirty seven	somthuml∂y siri
thirty eight	somthuml∂y kirit
thirty nine	somthuml∂y ku
fourty	somli
fourty one	somli l∂y kh∂t
fourty two	somli l∂y ni
fourty three	somli l∂y thum
fourty four	somli l∂y m∂li

fourty five	somli ləy raŋa
fourty six	somli ləy kuruk
fourty seven	somli ləy siri
fourty eight	somli ləy kirit
fourty nine	somli ləy ni
fifty	somŋa
fifty one	somŋa khət
fifty two	somŋa ləy ni
fifty three	somŋa ləy thum
fifty four	somŋa ləy məli
fifty five	somŋa ləy raŋa
fifty six	somŋa ləy kuruk
fifty seven	somŋa ləy siri
fifty eight	somŋa ləy kirit
fifty nine	somŋa ləy ku
sixty	somruk
sixty one	somruk ləy kht
sixty two	somruk ləy ni
sixty three	somruk ləy thum
sixty four	somruk ləy məli
sixty five	somruk ləy raŋa
sixty six	somruk ləy kuruk
sixty seven	somruk ləy siri
sixty eight	somruk ləy kirit
sixty nine	somruk ləy ku
seventy	somri
seventy one	somri ləy khət
seventy two	somri ləy ni
seventy three	somri ləy thum
seventy four	somri ləy məli
seventy five	somri ləy raŋa
seventy six	somri ləy kuruk

seventy seven	somri ləy siri
seventy eight	somri ləy kirit
seventy nine	somri ləy ni
eighty	somrit
eighty one	somrit ləy khət
eighty two	somrit ləy ni
eighty three	somrit ləy thum
eighty four	somrit ləy məli
eighty five	somrit ləy raŋa
eighty six	somrit ləy kuruk
eighty seven	somrit ləy siri
eighty eight	somrit ləy kirit
eighty nine	somrit ləy ku
ninety	somku
ninety one	somku ləy khət
ninety two	somku ləy ni
ninety three	somku ləy thum
ninety four	somku ləy məli
ninety five	somku ləy raŋa
ninety six	somku ləy kuruk
ninety seven	somku ləy siri
ninety eight	somku ləy kirit
ninety nine	somku ləy ku
one hundred	rəyya
two hundred	cəni
three hundred	rəyyathum
four hundred	rəyya məli
five hundred	rəyya raŋa
six hundred	rəyya kuruk
seven hundred	rəyya siri
eight hundred	rəyya kirit
nine hundred	rəyya ku

thousand	lisiŋ
two thousand	lisiŋ ni
three thousand	lisiŋ thum
four thousand	lisiŋ məli
five thousand	lisiŋ raŋa
six thousand	lisiŋ kuruk
seven thousand	lisŋ siri
eight thousand	lisiŋ kirit
nine thousand	lisiŋ ku
ten thousand	lisiŋ som

Ordinal number

first	məsət
second	nitipi
third	thumtipi
fourth	məlitipi
fifth	raŋatipi
sixth	kuruktipi
seventh	sisitipi
eighth	kirittipi
nineth	kutipi
tenth	tipi

APPENDIX III

Additional Vocabulary

ask	r∂y
ax	r∂y
arrest	∂sur
anger	saw
bed	kaŋthol
beat	khon
beno	bens
break	kh∂y
bye	inthrek
buy	l∂y
bring	thlen
broken	∂k∂y
blow	khiraŋ
can	cek
come	thleŋ, wa
cold	kisik
curry	∂n
clean	thlen
cut	nitan
cloth	pun
cook	sun
child	sa
dance	lam
do	tlo
duty	th∂w
end	ci

every	kumrel
fly	kejuŋ
fetch	icoy
flower	r∂y
fine	elen
fresh	∂kriŋ, green
give	pek
grainery house	tom
hungry	tram
heavy	kirik
help	paŋ
happy	haraw
insect	tuŋeŋ
inside	suŋ
insult	jak
kick	kaw
leaf	thor
leave	suti
look	∂n
may	∂ya
milk	cu, saŋgom
mosquito	luŋeŋ
nice	kathra
new	n∂w
now	epek
on	cuŋ
out	thru
pepper	siriŋ
peddy	inro
place	m∂ph∂m
permission	∂ya
picture	sinema
prepare	sem

reward	mƏna
read	pa
reap (v)	wat
ripe (v)	min
root	tuŋ
road	lam
run	∈ lan
sleep	in
small	Ərkdi
say	san
song	la
school	sakul
scold	Əsal
sing	thlo
sit	imbok
shadow	lip
stop	doŋ
stone	luŋ
shirt	luŋlut
tea	ca
throw	nilon
thief	inru
tiger	yukpi
thank	inthak
thread	ray
tree	thŋ
thatch	patdi
ugly	thi
win	thoy
withere	akaŋ
wash	katra

BIBLIOGRAPHY

Chhangte, Lalnunthangi, 1986. A Preliminary Grammar of Mizo Language (Unpublished M.A. Dissertation, University of Texas at Arlington.

_____. 'The grammar of simple clauses in Mizo' In Press in South East Asian Linguistics, 93-174, Pacific Linguistics. Ed. David Bradly.

Cornyn, W.S. and H.D. Roof 1968 Beginning Burmese. Yale University Press.

Sharma, D.D. 1988. A Descriptive Grammar of Kinnauri. Mittal Publications, Delhi.

Matisoff, James, A. 1973. The Grammar of Lahu. University of California Press, Berkeley.

Singh, Chungkham Yashawanta, 2000. Manipuri Grammar, Rajesh Publications, Delhi.